KU-675-361

ntents

White-sand beaches backed by coconut palms, steep winding streets lined with pastel-coloured houses, ornate baroque churches, Afro-Brazilian ceremonies, gymnastic martial art ballet, the rhythm of the *berimbau*, the aroma of spices … Bahia conjures up as many exotic images, sounds and smells as Rio de Janeiro and has as an equally strong claim to be the heart of Brazil. The state capital, Salvador, was the country's first city for far longer than any other, and is considered by many to be the country's cultural centre.

Brazil's most famous novelist, Jorge Amado, was a Bahian, as were many of its greatest musicians; it was Bahia that gave the world samba, capoeira, Carnaval and *candomblé*. The state has some of the best cuisine in the country, along with many of its best beaches. Bahia's beautiful coast stretches far to the north and south of Salvador and is dotted with resorts along its length: laid-back little places like Itacaré, Morro de São Paulo and Trancoso, and larger more hedonistic party-towns like Porto Seguro and Arraial da Ajuda. Inland, in the wild semi-desert of the *sertão*, is one of Brazil's premier hiking destinations, the Chapada Diamantina, whose towering escarpments are cut by clear-water rivers and dotted with plunging waterfalls.

Planning your trip

Best time to visit Salvador and Bahia

It can rain at any time of year in Bahia, but the main rainy season is between May and September. The climate is usually pleasant and the sun is never far away. Temperatures range from 25°C to 32°C, rarely falling below 19°C in winter. Humidity is relatively high in Brazil, particularly along the coast. The luminosity is also very high, and sunglasses are advised.

Business visitors should avoid mid-December to the end of February, when people are on holiday. In these months, hotels, beaches and transport tend to be very crowded. July is a school holiday month. Some tourist sights may be closed in low season. **Carnaval** is a movable feast, running for five riotous days from the Friday afternoon before Shrove Tuesday to the morning hangover of Ash Wednesday. For Carnaval dates, see page 50.

Getting to Salvador and Bahia

Air
Flights into Brazil usually arrive at **Cumbica International Airport** at Guarulhos (which is often used as an alternative name) in São Paulo, or **Tom Jobim International Airport** (also known as Galeão) on the Ilha do Governador, 16 km from the centre of Rio de Janeiro. From here there are onward flights to Salvador. Many other Brazilian cities have connections to the USA and Europe including Recife and Belo Horizonte. Salvador has international connections with Miami, Madrid, Frankfurt and Lisbon.

Prices are cheapest in October, November and after Carnaval and at their highest in the European summer and the Brazilian high seasons (generally 15 December to 15 January, the Thursday before Carnaval to the Saturday after Carnaval, and 15 June to 15 August). Departure tax is usually included in the cost of the ticket.

Air passes TAM and GOL offer a 21-day **Brazil Airpass**, which is valid on any TAM destination within Brazil. The price varies according to the number of flights taken and the international airline used to arrive in Brazil. They can only be bought outside Brazil. Rates vary depending on the season. Children pay a discounted rate; those under three pay 10% of the adult rate. Some of the carriers operate a blackout period between 15 December and 15 January.

Baggage allowance Airlines will only allow a certain weight of luggage without a surcharge; for Brazil this is usually two items of 32 kg but may be as low as 20 kg; with two items of hand luggage weighing up to 10 kg in total. UK airport staff can refuse to load bags weighing more than 30 kg. Baggage allowances are higher in business and first class. Weight limits for internal flights are often lower, usually 20 kg. In all cases it is best to enquire beforehand.

Transport in Salvador and Bahia

Public transport in Brazil is very efficient, but distances are huge. Most visitors will find themselves travelling by buses and planes, except in the Amazon when a boat is often the only way to get around. Train routes are practically non-existent, car hire is expensive and hitchhiking not advisable. Taxis vary widely in quality and price but are easy to come by and safe when taken from a *posto de taxis* (taxi rank).

Air

Because of the size of the country, flying is often the most practical option and internal air services are highly developed. All state capitals and larger cities are linked with each other with services several times a day, and all national airlines offer excellent service. Recent deregulation of the airlines has greatly reduced prices on some routes and low-cost airlines offer fares that can often be as cheap as travelling by bus (when booked through the internet). Paying with an international credit card is not always possible online; but it is usually possible to buy an online ticket through a hotel, agency or willing friend without surcharge. Many of the smaller airlines go in and out of business sporadically. **Avianca** ⓘ *www.avianca.com.br*, **Azul** ⓘ *www.voeazul.com.br*, **GOL** ⓘ *www.voegol.com.br*, **TAM** ⓘ *www.tam.com.br*, and **TRIP** ⓘ *www.voetrip.com.br*, operate the most extensive routes.

Road

The best paved highways are heavily concentrated in the southeast, but roads serving the interior are being improved to all-weather status and many are paved. Most main roads between principal cities are paved. Some are narrow and therefore dangerous; many are in poor condition.

Bus There are three standards of bus: *Comum*, or *Convencional*, are quite slow, not very comfortable and fill up quickly; *Executivo* are more expensive, comfortable (many have reclining seats), and don't stop en route to pick up passengers so are safer; *leito* (literally 'bed') run at night between the main centres, offering reclining seats with leg rests, toilets, and sometimes refreshments, at double the normal fare. For journeys over 100 km, most buses have chemical toilets (bring toilet paper). Air conditioning can make buses cold at night, so take a jumper; on some services blankets are supplied.

Buses stop fairly frequently (every two to four hours) at *postos* for snacks. Bus stations for interstate services and other long-distance routes are called *rodoviárias*. They are frequently outside the city centres and offer snack bars, lavatories, left luggage, local bus services and information centres. Buy bus tickets at *rodoviárias* (most now take credit cards), not from travel agents who add on surcharges. Reliable bus information is hard to come by, other than from companies themselves. Buses usually arrive and depart in very good time. Many town buses have turnstiles, which can be inconvenient if you are carrying a large pack. Urban buses normally serve local airports.

Car hire Renting a car in Brazil is expensive: the cheapest rate for unlimited mileage for a small car is about US$65 per day. These costs can be more than halved by reserving a car over the internet through one of the larger international companies such as **Europcar** (www.europcar.co.uk) or **Avis** (www.avis.co.uk). The minimum age for renting a car is 21 and it's essential to have a credit card. Companies operate under the terms *aluguel de automóveis* or *auto-locadores*. Check exactly what the company's insurance policy covers. In many cases it will not cover major accidents or 'natural' damage (eg flooding). Ask if extra cover is available. Sometimes using a credit card automatically includes insurance. Beware of being billed for scratches that were on the vehicle before you hired it.

Taxi Rates vary from city to city, but are consistent within each city. At the outset, make sure the meter is cleared and shows 'tariff 1', except (usually) from 2300-0600, Sunday, and in December when '2' is permitted. Check that the meter is working; if not, fix the price in advance. The **radio taxi** service costs about 50% more but cheating is less likely. Taxis outside larger hotels usually cost more. If you are seriously cheated, note the number of the taxi and insist on a signed bill; threatening to take it to the police can work. **Mototaxis** are much more economical, but many are unlicensed and there have been a number of robberies of passengers.

Where to stay in Salvador and Bahia

There is a good range of accommodation options in Brazil. An *albergue* or hostel offers the cheapest option. These have dormitory beds and single and double rooms. Many are part of the **IYHA** ① *www.iyha.org*. **Hostel World** ① *www.hostelworld.com*; **Hostel Bookers** ① *www.hostelbookers.com*; and **Hostel.com** ① *www.hostel.com*, are useful portals. **Hostel Trail Latin America** ① *T0131-208 0007 (UK), www.hosteltrail.com*, managed from their hostel in Popayan, is an online network of hotels and tour companies in South America. A *pensão* is either a cheap guesthouse or a household that rents out some rooms.

Pousadas
A *pousada* is either a bed-and-breakfast, often small and family-run, or a sophisticated and often charming small hotel. A *hotel* is as it is anywhere else in the world, operating according to the international star system, although five-star hotels are not price controlled and hotels in any category are not always of the standard of their star equivalent in the USA, Canada or Europe. Many of the older hotels can be cheaper than hostels. Usually accommodation prices include a breakfast of rolls, ham, cheese, cakes and fruit with coffee and juice; there is no reduction if you don't eat it. Rooms vary too. Normally an *apartamento* is a room with separate living and sleeping areas and sometimes cooking facilities. A *quarto* is a standard room; *com banheiro* is en suite; and *sem banheiro* is with shared bathroom. Finally there are the *motels*. These should not be confused with their US counterpart: motels are used by guests not intending to sleep; there is no stigma attached and they usually offer good value (the rate for a full night is called the '*pernoite*'), however the decor can be a little garish.

It's a good idea to book accommodation in advance in small towns that are popular at weekends with city dwellers, and it's essential to book at peak times. **Hidden Pousadas Brazil** ① *www.hiddenpousadasbrazil.com*, offers a range of the best *pousadas* around the country.

Luxury accommodation

Much of the best private accommodation sector can be booked through operators. **Angatu**, www.angatu.com, offers a range of private homes throughout Brazil, together with bespoke trips. **Matuete**, www.matuete.com, has a range of luxurious properties and tours.

Camping

Those with an international camping card pay only half the rate of a non-member at **Camping Clube do Brasil** sites ① *www.campingclube.com.br*. Membership of the club itself is expensive: US$90 for six months. The club has 43 sites in 13 states and 80,000 members. It may be difficult to get into some Camping Clube campsites during high season (January to February). Private campsites charge about US$10-15 per person. For those on a very low budget and in isolated areas where there is no campsite available, it's usually possible to stay at service stations. They have shower facilities, watchmen and food; some have dormitories. There are also various municipal sites. Campsites tend to be some distance from public transport routes and are better suited to people with their own car. Wild camping is generally difficult and dangerous. Never camp at the side of a road; this is very risky.

Homestays

Staying with a local family is an excellent way to become integrated quickly into a city and companies try to match guests to their hosts. **Cama e Café** ① *www.camaecafe.com. br*, organizes homestays in a number of other cities around Brazil. **Couch surfing** ① *www. couchsurfing.com*, offers a free, backpacker alternative.

Quality hotel associations

The better international hotel associations have members in Brazil. These include: **Small Luxury Hotels of the World** ① *www.slh.com*; the **Leading Hotels of the World** ① *www. lhw.com*; the **Leading Small Hotels of the World** ① *www.leadingsmallhotelsoftheworld. com*; **Great Small Hotels** ① *www.greatsmallhotels.com*; and the French group **Relais et Chateaux** ① *www.relaischateaux.com*, which also includes restaurants.

The Brazilian equivalent of these associations are **Hidden Pousadas Brazil** ① *www.hiddenpousadasbrazil.com*, and their associate, **Roteiros de Charme** ① *www. roteirosdecharme.com.br*. Membership of these groups pretty much guarantees quality, but it is by no means comprehensive.

Online travel agencies (OTAs)

Services like www.tripadvisor.com and OTAs associated with them – such as www.hotels.com, www.expedia.com and www.venere.com, are well worth using for both reviews and for booking ahead. Hotels booked through an OTA can be up to 50% cheaper than the rack rate. Similar sites operate for hostels (though discounts are far less considerable). They include the Hostelling International site, www.hihostels.com, www.hostelbookers.com, www.hostels.com and www.hostelworld.com.

Food and drink in Salvador and Bahia

Food → *See box, page 45, for more details of Bahian cuisine.*

While Brazil has some of the best fine dining restaurants in Latin America, everyday Brazilian cuisine – particularly in the southeast can be stolid. Mains are generally heavy, meaty and unspiced. Desserts are often very sweet. In the big cities, a heady mix of international immigrants has resulted in some unusual fusion cooking and exquisite variations on French, Japanese, Portuguese, Arabic and Italian traditional techniques and dishes and the regional cooking can be a delight. However, at times it can be a struggle to find interesting food. The Brazilian staple meal generally consists of a cut of fried or barbecued meat, chicken or fish accompanied by rice, black or South American broad beans and an unseasoned salad of lettuce, grated carrot, tomato and beetroot. Condiments consist of weak chilli sauce, olive oil, salt and pepper and vinegar.

The national dish is a greasy campfire stew called *feijoada*, made by throwing jerked beef, smoked sausage, tongue and salt pork into a pot with lots of fat and beans and stewing it for hours. The resulting stew is sprinkled with fried *farofa* (manioc flour) and served with *couve* (kale) and slices of orange. The meal is washed down with *cachaça* (sugarcane rum). Most restaurants serve the *feijoada completa* for Saturday lunch (up until about 1630). Come with a very empty stomach.

Brazil's other national dish is mixed grilled meat or *churrasco*, served in vast portions off the spit by legions of rushing waiters, and accompanied by a buffet of salads, beans and mashed vegetables. *Churrascos* are served in *churrascarias* or *rodízios*. The meat is generally excellent, especially in the best *churascarias*, and the portions are unlimited, offering good value for camel-stomached carnivores able to eat one meal a day.

In remembrance of Portugal, but bizarrely for a tropical country replete with fish, Brazil is also the world's largest consumer of cod, pulled from the cold north Atlantic, salted and served in watery slabs or little balls as *bacalhau* (an appetizer/bar snack) or *petisco*. Other national *petiscos* include *kibe* (a deep-fried or baked mince with onion, mint and flour), *coxinha* (deep-fried chicken or meat in dough), *empadas* (baked puff-pastry patties with prawns, chicken, heart of palm or meat), and *tortas* (little pies with the same ingredients). When served in bakeries, *padarias* or snack bars these are collectively referred to as *salgadinhos* (savouries).

The best cooking in Brazil is not national but regional. **Bahia** offers an African-infused, welcome break from meat, rice and beans further south, with a variety of seafood dishes. Unlike most Brazilians, Bahians have discovered sauces, pepper and chilli. The most famous Bahian dish is *moqueca* (fresh fish cooked slowly with prawns in *dendê* palm oil, coconut milk, garlic, tomatoes, cilantro and chili pepper).

Eating cheaply The cheapest dish is the *prato feito* or *sortido*, an excellent-value set menu usually comprising meat/chicken/fish, beans, rice, chips and salad. The *prato comercial* is similar but rather better and a bit more expensive. Portions are usually large enough for two and come with two plates. If you are on your own, you could ask for an *embalagem* (doggy bag) or a *marmita* (takeaway) and offer it to a person with no food (many Brazilians do). Many restaurants serve *comida por kilo* buffets where you serve yourself and pay for the weight of food on your plate. This is generally good value and is a good option for vegetarians. *Lanchonetes* and *padarias* (diners and bakeries) are good for cheap eats, usually serving *prato feitos*, *salgadinhos*, excellent juices and other snacks.

The main meal is usually taken in the middle of the day; cheap restaurants tend not to be open in the evening.

Drink

The national liquor is *cachaça* (also known as *pinga*), which is made from sugar-cane, and ranging from cheap supermarket and service-station fire-water, to boutique distillery and connoisseur labels from the interior of Minas Gerais. Mixed with fruit juice, sugar and crushed ice, *cachaça* becomes the principal element in a *batida*, a refreshing but deceptively powerful drink. Served with pulped lime or other fruit, mountains of sugar and smashed ice it becomes the world's favourite party cocktail, caipirinha. A less potent caipirinha made with vodka is called a *caipiroska* and with sake a *saikirinha* or *caipisake*.

Some genuine Scotch whisky brands are bottled in Brazil. They are far cheaper even than duty free; Teacher's is the best. Locally made and cheap gin, vermouth and campari are pretty much as good as their US and European counterparts.

Wine is becoming increasingly popular and Brazil is the third most important wine producer in South America. The wine industry is mainly concentrated in the south of the country where the conditions are most suitable, with over 90% of wine produced in Rio Grande do Sul. Reasonable national table wines include Château d'Argent, Château Duvalier, Almadén, Dreher, Preciosa and more respectable Bernard Taillan, Marjolet from Cabernet grapes, and the Moselle-type white Zahringer. There are some interesting sparkling wines in the Italian spumante style (the best is Casa Valduga Brut Premium Sparkling Wine), and Brazil produces still wines using many international and imported varieties. The best bottle of red is probably the Boscato Reserva Cabernet Sauvignon, but it's expensive (at around US$20 a bottle); you'll get far higher quality and better value buying Portuguese, Argentine or Chilean wines in Brazil.

Brazilian beer is generally lager, served ice-cold. Draught beer is called *chope* or *chopp* (after the German Schoppen, and pronounced 'shoppi'). There are various national brands of bottled beers, which include Brahma, Skol, Cerpa, Antartica and the best Itaipava and Bohemia. There are black beers too, notably Xingu. They tend to be sweet. The best beer is from the German breweries in Rio Grande do Sul and is available only there.

Brazil's myriad fruits are used to make fruit juices or *sucos*, which come in a delicious variety, unrivalled anywhere in the world. *Açai acerola*, *caju* (cashew), *pitanga*, *goiaba* (guava), *genipapo*, *graviola* (chirimoya), *maracujá* (passion fruit), *sapoti*, *umbu* and *tamarindo* are a few of the best. *Vitaminas* are thick fruit or vegetable drinks with milk. *Caldo de cana* is sugar-cane juice, sometimes mixed with ice. *Água de côco* or *côco verde* is coconut water served straight from a chilled, fresh, green coconut. The best known of many local soft drinks is *guaraná*, which is a very popular carbonated fruit drink, completely unrelated to the Amazon nut. The best variety is *guaraná Antarctica*. Coffee is ubiquitous and good tea entirely absent.

Responsible travel in Salvador and Bahia

Tourism is booming in Brazil. In recent years, growth in the hospitalities industry has forged thousands of new jobs and funnelled millions of dollars into the economy. Nonetheless, Brazil's burgeoning tourist scene has not always worked to the benefit of local communities – or the natural environment. Fortunately, there are some very dedicated environmentalists working in tourism and lobbying the government for greater awareness and change. As a visitor, you can make a significant difference at this critical stage in the country's development.

10 ways to be a responsible traveller
There are some aspects of travel that you have to accept are going to have an impact, but try to balance the negatives with positives by following these guidelines to responsible travel.

• **Cut your emissions** Plan an itinerary that minimizes carbon emissions whenever possible. This might involve travelling by train, hiring a bike or booking a walking or canoeing tour rather than one that relies on vehicle transport. See opposite page for details of carbon offset programmes. Visit www.seat61.com for worldwide train travel.

• **Check the small print** Choose travel operators that abide by a responsible travel policy (if they have one it will usually be posted on their website). Visit www.responsibletravel.com.

• **Keep it local** If travelling independently, try to use public transport, stay in locally owned accommodation, eat in local restaurants, buy local produce and hire local guides.

• **Cut out waste** Take biodegradable soap and shampoo and leave excess packaging, particularly plastics, at home. The countries you are visiting may not have the waste collection or recycling facilities to deal with it.

• **Get in touch** Find out if there are any local schools, charities or voluntary conservation organizations that you could include in your itinerary. If appropriate, take along some useful gifts or supplies; www.stuffyourrucksack.com has a list of projects that could benefit from your support.

• **Learn the lingo** Practise some local words, even if it's just to say 'hello', 'thank you' and 'goodbye'. Respect local customs and dress codes and always ask permission before photographing people – including your wildlife tour guide. Once you get home, remember to honour any promises you've made to send photographs.

• **Avoid the crowds** Consider travelling out of season to relieve pressure on popular destinations, or visit a lesser-known alternative.

• **Take only photos** Resist the temptation to buy souvenirs made from animals or plants. Not only is it illegal to import or export many wildlife souvenirs, but their uncontrolled collection supports poaching and can have a devastating impact on local populations, upsetting the natural balance of entire ecosystems.
   CITES, the Convention on International Trade in Endangered Species (www.cites.org) bans international trade in around 900 animal and plant species, and controls trade in a further 33,000 species.

Several organizations, including WWF, TRAFFIC and the Smithsonian Institution have formed the Coalition Against Wildlife Trafficking (www.cawtglobal.org).

• **Use water wisely** Water is a precious commodity. Treating your own water avoids the need to buy bottles which can contribute to the build-up of litter.

• **Don't interfere** Avoid disturbing wildlife, damaging habitats or interfering with natural behaviour by feeding wild animals, getting too close or being too noisy. Leave plants and shells where you find them.

Code green for hikers
• Take biodegradable soap, shampoo and toilet paper, long-lasting lithium batteries and plastic bags for packing out all rubbish.
• Use a water filter instead of buying bottled water and save fuel at remote lodges by ordering the same food at the same time. Only take a hot shower if the water has been heated by solar power.
• If no toilet facilities are available, make sure you are at least 30 m from any water source.
• Keep to trails to avoid erosion and trampling vegetation. Don't take short cuts, especially at high altitude where plants may take years to recover.

Code green for divers and snorkellers
• Help conserve underwater environments by joining local clean-ups or collecting data for Project AWARE (www.projectaware.org).
• Choose resorts that properly treat sewage and wastewater and support marine protected areas.
• Choose operators that use mooring

buoys or drift diving techniques, rather than anchors, which can damage fragile marine habitats such as coral reefs.
• Never touch coral. Practise buoyancy-control skills in a pool or sandy area before diving around coral reefs, and tuck away trailing equipment.
• Avoid handling or feeding marine life.
• Never purchase marine souvenirs.
• Don't order seafood caught using destructive or unsustainable practices such as dynamite fishing.

How should I offset my carbon emissions?
Carbon offsetting schemes allow you to offset greenhouse gas emissions by donating to various projects, from tree planting to renewable energy schemes. Although some conservation groups are concerned that carbon offsetting is being used as a smoke-screen to delay the urgent action needed to cut emissions and develop alternative energy solutions, it remains an important way of counterbalancing your carbon footprint.

For every tonne of CO_2 you generate through a fossil fuel-burning activity, such as flying, you pay for an equivalent tonne to be removed elsewhere through a 'green' initiative. There are numerous online carbon footprint calculators (such as www.carbonfootprint.com). Alternatively, book with a travel operator that supports a carbon offset provider like TICOS (www.ticos.co.uk) or Reduce my Footprint (www.reducemyfootprint.travel).

It's not all about tree-planting schemes. Support now goes to a far wider range of climate-friendly technology projects, from the provision of energy-efficient light bulbs and cookers to large-scale renewable energy schemes such as wind farms.

Essentials A-Z

Accident and emergency
Ambulance T192. **Police** T190. If robbed or attacked, contact the tourist police. If you need to claim on insurance, make sure you get a police report.

Electricity
Generally 110 V 60 cycles AC, but in some cities and areas 220 V 60 cycles AC is used. European and US 2-pin plugs and sockets.

Embassies and consulates
For embassies and consulates of Brazil, see www.embassiesabroad.com.

Health ➔ *Hospitals/medical services are listed in the Directory sections of each chapter.*
See your GP or travel clinic at least 6 weeks before departure for general advice on travel risks and vaccinations. Make sure you have sufficient medical travel insurance, get a dental check, know your own blood group and, if you suffer a long-term condition such as diabetes or epilepsy, obtain a **Medic Alert** bracelet (www.medicalalert.co.uk).

Vaccinations and anti-malarials
Confirm that your primary courses and boosters are up to date. It is advisable to vaccinate against polio, tetanus, typhoid, hepatitis A and, for more remote areas, rabies. Yellow fever vaccination is obligatory for most areas. Cholera, diptheria and hepatitis B vaccinations are sometimes advised. Seek specialist advice on the best antimalarials to take before you leave.

Health risks
The major risks posed in the region are those caused by insect disease carriers such as mosquitoes and sandflies. The key parasitic and viral diseases are malaria, South American trypanosomiasis (Chagas disease) and dengue fever. Be aware that you are always at risk from these diseases. **Malaria** is a danger throughout the lowland tropics and coastal regions. **Dengue fever** (which is currently rife in Rio de Janeiro state) is particularly hard to protect against as the mosquitoes can bite throughout the day as well as night (unlike those that carry malaria); try to wear clothes that cover arms and legs and also use effective mosquito repellent. Mosquito nets dipped in permethrin provide a good physical and chemical barrier at night. **Chagas disease** is spread by faeces of the triatomine, or assassin bugs, whereas sandflies spread a disease of the skin called **leishmaniasis**.

Some form of **diarrhoea** or intestinal upset is almost inevitable, the standard advice is always to wash your hands before eating and to be careful with drinking water and ice; if you have any doubts about the water then boil it or filter and treat it. In a restaurant buy bottled water or ask where the water has come from. Food can also pose a problem, be wary of salads if you don't know if it has been washed or not.

There is a constant threat of **tuberculosis** (TB) and although the BCG vaccine is available, it is still not guaranteed protection. It is best to avoid unpasteurized dairy products and try not to let people cough and splutter all over you.

Another risk, especially to campers and people with small children, is that of the **hanta virus**, which is carried by some forest and riverine rodents. Symptoms are a flu-like illness which can lead to complications. Try to avoid rodent-infested areas, especially close contact with droppings.

Money

Currency → £1 = 3.9; €1 = 3.3; US$1 = R$2.4 *(Feb 2014).*

The unit of currency is the *real*, R$ (plural **reais**). Any amount of foreign currency and 'a reasonable sum' in reais can be taken in, but sums over US$10,000 must be declared. Residents may only take out the equivalent of US$4000. Notes in circulation are: 100, 50, 10, 5 and 1 real; coins: 1 real, 50, 25, 10, 5 and 1 centavo. **Note** The exchange rate fluctuates – check regularly.

Costs of travelling

Brazil is more expensive than other countries in South America. As a very rough guide, prices are about two-thirds those of Western Europe and a little cheaper than rural USA.

Hostel beds are usually around US$15. Budget hotels with few frills have rooms for as little as US$30, and you should have no difficulty finding a double room costing US$45 wherever you are. Rooms are often pretty much the same price whether 1 or 2 people are staying. Eating is generally inexpensive, especially in *padarias* or *comida por kilo* (pay by weight) restaurants, which offer a wide range of food (salads, meat, pasta, vegetarian). Expect to pay around US$6 to eat your fill in a good-value restaurant. Although bus travel is cheap by US or European standards, because of the long distances, costs can soon mount up. Internal flights prices have come down dramatically in the last couple of years and some routes work out cheaper than taking a bus – especially if booking through the internet. Prices vary regionally. Ipanema is almost twice as expensive as rural Bahia.

ATMs

ATMs, or cash machines, are common in Brazil. As well as being the most convenient way of withdrawing money, they frequently offer the best available rates of exchange.

They are usually closed after 2130 in large cities. There are 2 international ATM acceptance systems, **Plus** and **Cirrus**. Many issuers of debit and credit cards are linked to one, or both (eg Visa is Plus, MasterCard is Cirrus). **Bradesco** and **HSBC** are the 2 main banks offering this service. **Red Banco 24 Horas** kiosks advertise that they take a long list of credit cards in their ATMs, including MasterCard and Amex, but international cards cannot always be used; the same is true of **Banco do Brasil**.

Advise your bank before leaving, as cards are usually stopped in Brazil without prior warning. Find out before you leave what international functionality your card has. Check if your bank or credit card company imposes handling charges. Internet banking is useful for monitoring your account or transferring funds. Do not rely on one card, in case of loss. If you do lose a card, immediately contact the 24-hr helpline of the issuer in your home country (keep this number in a safe place).

Exchange

Banks in major cities will change cash and traveller's cheques (TCs). If you keep the official exchange slips, you may convert back into foreign currency up to 50% of the amount you exchanged. The parallel market, found in travel agencies, exchange houses and among hotel staff, often offers marginally better rates than the banks but commissions can be very high. Many banks may only change US$300 minimum in cash, US$500 in TCs. Rates for TCs are usually far lower than for cash, they are harder to change and a very heavy commission may be charged.

Credit cards

Credit cards are widely used, athough often they are not usable in the most unlikely of places, such as tour operators. **Diners Club,**

MasterCard, Visa and Amex are useful. Cash advances on credit cards will only be paid in reais at the tourist rate, incurring at least a 1.5% commission. Banks in remote places may refuse to give a cash advance: try asking for the *gerente* (manager).

Opening hours
Generally Mon-Fri 0900-1800; closed for lunch sometime between 1130 and 1400. **Shops** Also open on Sat until 1230 or 1300. **Government offices** Mon-Fri 1100-1800. **Banks** Mon-Fri 1000-1600 or 1630; closed at weekends.

Safety
Although Brazil's big cities suffer high rates of violent crime, this is mostly confined to the *favelas* (slums) where poverty and drugs are the main cause. Visitors should not enter *favelas* except when accompanied by workers for NGOs, tour groups or other people who know the local residents well and are accepted by the community. Otherwise they may be targets of muggings by armed gangs who show short shrift to those who resist them. Mugging can take place anywhere. Travel light after dark with few valuables (avoid wearing jewellery and use a cheap, plastic, digital watch). Ask hotel staff where is and isn't safe; crime is patchy in Brazilian cities.

If the worst does happen and you are threatened, don't panic, and hand over your valuables. Do not resist, and report the crime to the local tourist police later. It is extremely rare for a tourist to be hurt during a robbery in Brazil. Being aware of the dangers, acting confidently and using your common sense will reduce many of the risks.

Photocopy your passport, air ticket and other documents, make a record of traveller's cheque and credit card numbers. Keep them separately from the originals and leave another set of records at home. Keep all documents secure; hide your main cash supply in different places or under your clothes. Extra pockets sewn inside shirts and trousers, money belts (best worn below the waist), neck or leg pouches and elasticated support bandages for keeping money above the elbow or below the knee have been repeatedly recommended.

All border areas should be regarded with some caution because of smuggling activities. Violence over land ownership in parts of the interior have resulted in a 'Wild West' atmosphere in some towns, which should therefore be passed through quickly. Red-light districts should also be given a wide berth as there are reports of drinks being drugged with a substance popularly known as 'good night Cinderella'. This leaves the victim easily amenable to having their possessions stolen, or worse.

Avoiding cons
Never trust anyone telling sob stories or offering 'safe rooms', and when looking for a hotel, always choose the room yourself. Be wary of 'plain-clothes policemen'; insist on seeing identification and on going to the police station by main roads. Do not hand over your identification (or money) until you are at the station. On no account take them directly back to your hotel. Be even more suspicious if they seek confirmation of their status from a passer-by.

Hotel security
Hotel safe deposits are generally, but not always, secure. If you cannot get a receipt for valuables in a hotel safe, you can seal the contents in a plastic bag and sign across the seal. Always keep an inventory of what you have deposited. If you don't trust the hotel, lock everything in your pack and secure it in your room when you go out. If you lose valuables, report to the police and note details of the report for insurance purposes. Be sure to be present whenever your credit card is used.

Police
There are several types of police: **Polícia Federal**, civilian dressed, who handle all

federal law duties, including immigration. A subdivision is the **Polícia Federal Rodoviária**, uniformed, who are the traffic police on federal highways. **Polícia Militar** are the uniformed, street police force, under the control of the state governor, handling all state laws. They are not the same as the Armed Forces' internal police. **Polícia Civil**, also state controlled, handle local laws and investigations. They are usually in civilian dress, unless in the traffic division. In cities, the *prefeitura* controls the **Guarda Municipal**, who handle security. **Tourist police** operate in places with a strong tourist presence. In case of difficulty, visitors should seek out tourist police in the first instance.

Public transport
When you have all your luggage with you at a bus or railway station, be especially careful and carry any shoulder bags in front of you. To be extra safe, take a taxi between the airport/bus station/railway station and hotel, keep your bags with you and pay only when you and your luggage are outside; avoid night buses and arriving at your destination at night.

Sexual assault
If you are the victim of a sexual assault, you are advised firstly to contact a doctor (this can be your home doctor). You will need tests to determine whether you have contracted any STDs; you may also need advice on emergency contraception. You should contact your embassy, where consular staff will be very willing to help.

Telephone → Country code: +55.
Ringing: equal tones with long pauses. Engaged: equal tones, equal pauses.

Making a phone call in Brazil can be confusing. It is necessary to dial a 2-digit telephone company code prior to the area code for all calls. Phone numbers are now printed in this way: 0XX71 (0 for a national call, XX for the code of the phone company chosen (eg 31 for Telemar) followed by '71'

for Salvador, for example, and the 8-digit number of the subscriber. The same is true for international calls where 00 is followed by the operator code and then the country code and number.

Time
Brazil has 4 time zones: Brazilian standard time is GMT-3. Clocks move forward 1 hr in summer for approximately 5 months (usually between Oct and Feb or Mar), but times of change vary.

Tipping
Tipping is not usual, but always appreciated as staff are often paid a pittance. In restaurants, add 10% of the bill if no service charge is included; cloakroom attendants deserve a small tip; porters have fixed charges but often receive tips as well; unofficial car parkers on city streets should be tipped R$2.

Tourist information
The **Ministério do Turismo**, Esplanada dos Ministérios, Bloco U, 2nd and 3rd floors, Brasília, www.turismo.gov.br or www.brazil tour.com, is in charge of tourism in Brazil and has information in many languages. **Embratur**, the Brazilian Institute of Tourism, is at the same address, and is in charge of promoting tourism abroad. For information and phone numbers for your country visit **www.braziltour.com**. Local tourist information bureaux are not usually helpful for information on cheap hotels – they generally just dish out pamphlets. Telephone directories (not Rio) contain good street maps.

Other good sources of information are: **LATA**, www.lata.org. The Latin American Travel Association, with useful country information and listings of all UK operators specializing in Latin America. Also has up-to-date information on public safety, health, weather, travel costs, economics and politics highlighted for each nation. Wide selection of Latin American maps available, as well as individual travel planning assistance.

South American Explorers, formerly the **South American Explorers Club**, 126 Indina Creek Rd, Ithaca, NY 14850, T607-277 0488, www.samexplo.org. A non-profit organization functioning primarily as an information network for South America.

National parks

National parks are run by the Brazilian institute of environmental protection, **Ibama**, SCEN Trecho 2, Av L-4 Norte, Edif Sede de Ibama, CEP 70818-900, Brasília, DF, T061-3316 1212, www.ibama.gov.br. For information, contact **Linha Verde**, T0800-618080, linhaverde.sede@ibama.gov.br. National parks are open to visitors, usually with a permit from Ibama. See also the **Ministério do Meio Ambiente** website, www.mma.gov.br.

Visas and immigration

Visas are not required for stays of up to 90 days by tourists from Andorra, Argentina, Austria, Bahamas, Barbados, Belgium, Bolivia, Chile, Colombia, Costa Rica, Denmark, Ecuador, Finland, France, Germany, Greece, Iceland, Ireland, Italy, Liechtenstein, Luxembourg, Malaysia, Monaco, Morocco, Namibia, the Netherlands, Norway, Paraguay, Peru, Philippines, Portugal, San Marino, South Africa, Spain, Suriname, Sweden, Switzerland, Thailand, Trinidad and Tobago, United Kingdom, Uruguay, the Vatican and Venezuela. For them, only the following documents are required at the port of disembarkation: a passport valid for at least 6 months (or *cédula de identidad* for nationals of Argentina, Chile, Paraguay and Uruguay); and a return or onward ticket, or adequate proof that you can purchase your return fare, subject to no remuneration being received in Brazil and no legally binding or contractual documents being signed. Venezuelan passport holders can stay for 60 days on filling in a form at the border.

Citizens of the USA, Canada, Australia, New Zealand and other countries not mentioned above, and anyone wanting to stay longer than 180 days, *must* get a visa before arrival, which may, if you ask, be granted for multiple entry. US citizens must be fingerprinted on entry to Brazil. Visa fees vary from country to country, so apply to the Brazilian consulate in your home country. The consular fee in the USA is US$55. Students planning to study in Brazil or employees of foreign companies can apply for a 1- or 2-year visa. 2 copies of the application form, 2 photos, a letter from the sponsoring company or educational institution in Brazil, a police form showing no criminal convictions and a fee of around US$80 is required.

Identification

You must always carry identification when in Brazil. Take a photocopy of the personal details in your passport, plus your Brazilian immigration stamp, and leave your passport in the hotel safe deposit. This photocopy, when authorized in a *cartório*, US$1, is a legitimate copy of your documents. Be prepared, however, to present the originals when travelling in sensitive border areas. Always keep an independent record of your passport details. Also register with your consulate to expedite document replacement if yours gets lost or stolen.

Warning Do not lose the entry/exit permit they give you when you enter Brazil. Leaving the country without it, you may have to pay up to US$100 per person. It is suggested that you photocopy this form and have it authenticated at a *cartório*, US$1, in case of loss or theft.

Weights and measures

Metric.

Contents

Footprint features

At a glance

⊖ **Getting around** Buses and internal flights. Car hire a possibility for the coast.

◐ **Time required** 2-3 days for Salvador; 5 days for Salvador and beaches; 7-10 days for Salvador, the Chapada Diamantina and beaches.

☼ **Weather** Varies greatly over such a large region. Hot summer (Oct-Mar), warm winter (Apr-Sep). Hot and dry in the *sertão* all year round except Dec-Feb.

✕ **When not to go** Apr-May and Nov-Dec are wettest on the coast. Dec-Feb are wet in the *chapada*.

Salvador & Bahia

Salvador and the Recôncavo

Salvador is the capital not just of Bahia but of African Brazil. The country's African heritage is at its strongest here – in the ubiquitous *Orixá* spirit gods and goddesses, the carnival rhythms of the drum troupe orchestras of Ilê Aiyê and Olodum, the rich spicy cooking, the rituals of *candomblé* (Brazil's equivalent of *santeria*) and in the martial art ballet of capoeira. You will see the latter being performed on Salvador's beaches and in the squares and cobbled streets of the city's historical centre, the Pelourinho. The Pelourinho is also home to one of the most impressive collections of colonial architecture in South America. There are myriad baroque churches here. Some, like the Convento do São Francisco, have interiors covered with tons of gold plate. Others, like Nossa Senhora do Rosário, are decorated with statues of black saints and art that celebrates African Brazilian culture. The city is famous for its frenetic carnival which, unlike Rio's, takes place in the streets to the pounding rhythms of *axé* music. The crowds are overwhelming and move like a human wave.

The Baía de Todos os Santos is Brazil's largest bay and is dotted with islands; many of them are privately owned, others serve as weekend resorts for people from Salvador. The best known is Itaparica, a long, thin island lined with palms, with a pretty colonial capital and some reasonable beaches. Many buses run from here, and taking the ferry across from Salvador and then road transport from Itaparica is the quickest way to get to southern Bahia.

Behind the bay is the Recôncavo, a fertile hinterland where agriculture in Brazil was born – and where hundreds of thousands of indigenous Brazilians and enslaved Africans sweated and died to harvest sugar cane, cocoa and coffee. It is dotted with sleepy colonial towns, the most famous of which are Cachoeira and its twin across the Rio Paraguaçu, São Felix.

Arriving in Salvador and the Recôncavo → *For listings, see pages 40-56.*

Phone code: 071. Population: 3.2 million.

Getting there

Air Domestic and international flights arrive at **Luís Eduardo Magalhães Airport** ⓘ *28 km east of the centre, Praça Gago Coutinho, São Cristóvão, T071-3204 1010, www. aeroportosalvador.net*, previously known as Dois de Julho. There are ATM machines and a branch of Banco do Brasil on the ground floor. The tourist information booth (open 24 hours, English-speaking), has a list of hotels and a useful map. Buses link the airport with the city. Aeroporto (Linha S002-00) buses run from the airport to the historic centre (Praça da Sé) every 30 minutes (Monday to Friday 0500-2200, weekends 0600-2200, US$1.50) via Rio Vermelho, Barra and the city beaches. Other bairros are also served; see

1 Salvador orientation

Where to stay 🛏
Catharina Paraguaçu 1
Ibis 2
Pestana Bahia 3
Zank 4

➡ Salvador maps
1 Salvador orientation, page 21
2 Salvador centre, page 25
3 Pelourinho, page 30
4 Salvador south to Barra, page 34

www.transalvador.salvador.ba.gov.br for details. Fixed-rate taxis go both to Barra and the centre; tickets can be bought from the desk next to the tourist information booth) for around US$45. Ordinary taxis leave from outside the airport, US$35.

Bus Interstate buses arrive at the **rodoviária** ① *5 km east of the centre, near Iguatemi Shopping Centre, www.rodoviariaonline.com.br.* There are regular bus services to the centre (see www.transalvador.salvador.ba.gov.br), Campo Grande, Barra and Rio Vermelho (marked Praça da Sé/Centro). An executive bus leaves from outside the shopping centre (reached from the bus station by a walkway; be careful at night) and runs to Praça da Sé or the lower city (Comércio) via the coast road. A taxi to the centre costs around US$25. ▶ *See Transport, page 53.*

Ferries and catamarans The main ferry dock, principally for car ferries although also for catamarans and passenger boats, is the **Marítimo de São Joaquim** ① *Av Oscar Pontes 1051, T071-3254 1020.* It is known colloquially as 'ferry-boat' (pronounced 'fairhee bort)'. The terminal has a bank, cafés and some small shops. Ten car ferries per day arrive here from the little town of Bom Despacho on Itaparica.

Salvador's other boat terminal is smaller and serves only passengers. It lies opposite the Mercado Modelo, five minutes' walk from the historic centre, and is known as the **Terminal Marítimo de Mercado Modelo** or **Terminal Marítimo Turistico**. Ferries and catamarans run between here and the Baía de Todos os Santos, including the village of Mar Grande on Itaparica (every 30 minutes) and there are catamarans from Morro de São Paulo (five a day in high season; three in low season; the last leaves at 1400, 2½ hours, www.biotur.com.br).

Getting around

The city is built on a broad peninsula and is at the mouth of the Baía de Todos os Santos. On the opposite side of the bay's entrance is the Ilha de Itaparica (see page 37). The commercial district of the city and its port are on the sheltered western side of the peninsula; residential districts and beaches are on the open Atlantic side. Barra lies at the point of the peninsula.

The centre of the city is divided into two levels, the **Cidade Alta** (Upper City) where the historic centre and Pelourinho lies, and the **Cidade Baixa** (Lower City), which is the commercial and docks district. The two levels are connected by a series of steep hills called *ladeiras*. The easiest way to go from one level to the other is by the Lacerda Lift, which connects Praça Municipal (Tomé de Sousa) in the Upper City with Praça Cairu and the famous Mercado Modelo market. The *Plano Inclinado Gonçalves* funicular railway leaves from behind the cathedral and runs to Comércio, the commercial district of the lower city near the market (US$0.15). The Plano Inclinado do Pilar funicular runs from next to the **Pousada do Pilar** in Santo Antonio to the Comércio (US$0.15). Airport bus services (see above for website and information) run between the historic centre, Barra and the beaches and are the best way to get around.

The **Salvador Bus** ① *T071-3356 6425, www.salvadorbus.com.br,* runs coach tours of the city with a commentary in Portuguese and English. Buses are air-conditioned on the lower deck and open-topped above (with a covering for when it rains) and call at Rio Vermelho, Orla Marítima (esplanade), Farol da Barra lighthouse and beach, the forts, Museu de Arte da Bahia, Praça Castro Alves, the Pelourinho, Elevador Lacerda, Igreja do Bonfim, Solar de Unhão and Museu de Arte Moderna, and Dique do Tororó. They are hop-on/hop-off with a wristband ticket (US$22.50, US$15 for children aged seven to 12). Five buses a day are scheduled (currently 0830-1900) though in reality the service is sporadic and unpredictable. Tickets can be bought at travel agencies, hotels, commercial centres, **Iguatemi Shopping** (Salvador) and on the buses themselves.

Most visitors limit themselves to the centre, Barra, the Atlantic suburbs and the Itapagipe Peninsula, which is north of the centre. The roads and avenues between these areas are straightforward to follow and are well served by public transport. Other parts of the city are not as easy to get around, but are of less interest to most visitors. If you go to these areas, a taxi may be advisable until you are familiar with Salvador. The website www.transalvador. salvador.ba.gov.br/transporte has details of bus routes in Salvador with a search facility and prices. Buses are fast and frequent. The main bus stop in the Centro Histórico is at the southern end of Praça Municipal (Tomé de Sousa). Buses from the city centre to Bonfim leave from Avenida da França near the Mercado Modelo. ▶▶ *See Transport, page 53.*

Tourist information

The main office of **Bahiatursa** ① *Av Simon Bolivar, 650, T071-3117 3000, www.bahiatursa. ba.gov.br, Mon-Fri 0830-1800,* has lists of hotels and accommodation in private homes, can advise on travel throughout the state of Bahia, and has noticeboards for messages. There are also branches at the following locations: **airport** ① *T071-3204 1244, daily 0730-2300;* **Mercado Modelo** ① *Praça Visconde de Cayru 250, T071-3241 0242, Mon-Sat 0900-1800, Sun 0900-1330;* **Pelourinho** ① *R das Laranjeiras 12, T071-3321 2133/2463, daily 0830-2100;* **Rodoviária** ① *T071-3450 3871, daily 0730-2100;* **Instituto Mauá** ① *Praça Azevedo Fernandes 1, Porto da Barra, T071-3264 4671, Mon-Fri 0900-1800, Sat 1000-1500;* **Shopping Barra** ① *Av Centenário, 2992, Chame-Chame, T071-3264 4566, Mon-Fri 0900-1900, Sat 0900-1400;* and **Shopping Iguatemi** ① *Av Tancredo Neves 148, Pituba, T071-3480 5511, Mon-Fri 0900-2130, Sat 0900-1330.* The website www.bahia-online.net lists cultural events and news.

Safety

There is a lot of paranoia about safety in Salvador but as long as visitors follow common sense and a few rules they should be fine. The civil police are helpful and Barra, the Pelourinho and the old part of the city are well lit at night with a strong police presence. The Pelourinho area is generally safe: there's plenty of begging/touting and watch out for pickpocketing, but muggings are rare (though they do occur, usually late at night). Be vigilant and do not use the Lacerda Lift and funiculars at night and do not go to the Comercio area of the Lower City after dark. Never venture into the *favelas* unless on a tour or with a trustworthy local friend. Women can receive unwelcome amounts of attention, especially during **Carnaval** when levels of physical contact in crowds can be unpleasant.

Background

On 1 November 1501, All Saints' Day, the navigator Amérigo Vespucci discovered the bay and named it after the day of his arrival – Baía de Todos os Santos. The bay was one of the finest anchorages on the coast and became a favourite port of call for French, Spanish and Portuguese ships. However, when the Portuguese crown sent Martim Afonso to set up a permanent colony in Brazil, he favoured São Vicente in São Paulo.

It was not until nearly 50 years later that the bay's strategic importance was recognized. When the first governor general, Tomé de Sousa, arrived on 23 March 1549 to build a fortified city to protect Portugal's interest from constant threats of Dutch and French invasion, the bay was chosen as the place from which the new colony of Brazil was to be governed. Salvador was formally founded on 1 November 1549 and, despite a short-lived Dutch invasion in 1624, remained the capital of Brazil until 1763.

The city grew wealthy through the export of sugar and the import of African slaves to work on the plantations. By the 18th century, it was the most important city in the Portuguese empire after Lisbon, and ideally situated on the main trade routes of the New World. Its fortunes were further boosted by the discovery of diamonds in the interior. However, as the sugar industry declined, the local economy could not rival the gold and coffee booms of the southeast and this led to the loss of capital status and the rise of Rio de Janeiro as Brazil's principal city. Nevertheless, the city continued to play an influential part in the political and cultural life of the country.

African presence

For three centuries, Salvador was the site of a thriving slave trade, with much of the workforce for the sugar cane and tobacco plantations coming from the west coast of Africa. Even today, Salvador is described as the most African city in the Western hemisphere, and the University of Bahia has the only choir in the Americas to sing in the Yoruba language. The influence permeates the city: food sold on the street is the same as in Senegal and Nigeria, the music is fused with pulsating African polyrhythms, men and women nonchalantly carry enormous loads on their heads, fishermen paddle dug-out canoes in the bay, and the pace of life is more relaxed than in other parts of the country.

Modern Salvador

Salvador today is a fascinating mixture of old and modern, rich and poor, African and European, religious and profane. The city has 15 forts, 166 Catholic churches and 1000 *candomblé* temples. It remains a major port, exporting tropical fruit, cocoa, sisal, soya beans and petrochemical products. However, its most important industry is tourism, and it is the second largest tourist attraction in the country, after Rio.

Local government has done much to improve the fortunes of this once rundown, poor and dirty city. Major investments are being made in its infrastructure and public health areas. A new comprehensive sewage system has been installed throughout the city, with a view to improving living conditions and dealing with pollution.

The once-forgotten Lower City, Ribeira and the Itapagipe Peninsula districts have received major facelifts. Major investments are being made by multinational firms in the automotive and petrochemical industries, principally in the Camaçari complex, 40 km from the city. The Bahian economy is currently the fastest growing in the country.

Centro Histórico → *For listings, see pages 40-56.*

Most of the interesting sights in Salvador are concentrated in the Centro Histórico in the **Cidade Alta** (Upper City). This is where the Portuguese founded the first capital of Brazil in November 1549. The entire 2-km stretch between the Praça Municipal in the south and the Carmelite churches (Carmo) in the north is a World Heritage Site.

This is the vibrant and colourful heart of Salvador. The colonial houses are painted in pastel colours, and many have been converted into restaurants, small hotels or bars, whose tables spill out onto the patios behind the houses; they host live music several times a week. The entire area proliferates with handicraft shops, artist ateliers and African-Brazilian cultural centres.

2 Salvador centre

To Forte Santo Antônio Além do Carmo

SANTO ANTÔNIO

N

200 metres
200 yards

Where to stay

Hostel Nega Maluca 9
O Convento do Carmo 7
Pousada do Boqueirão 3
Pousada do Pilar 5
Pousada Redfish 1
Pousada
 Santo Antônio 6
Pousada Villa Carmo 4

Restaurants

Al Carmo 1
Amado 2
SoHo 4

Funicular Plano
Inclinado Pilar

Largo do Cais
do Ouro

Carmo

Santíssimo
Sacramento
do Passo

Ordem Terceira
do Carmo

PELOURINHO

Buses for
Bonfim

Plano
Inclinado
Gonçalves

Largo de
Pelourinho

Catedral
Basílica

CIDADE
BAIXA

Terreiro
de Jesus

Ilha Bela
Transporte

Praça
da Sé

Mercado
Modelo

São Francisco

Terminal
Marítimo
Turístico
(Boats to
Itaparica &
Morro de
São Paulo)

Praça
Cairu

Praça
Municipal

Paço
Municipal

CENTRO

Lacerda
Lift

Palácio Rio
Branco

CIDADE
ALTA

NS da
Conceição
da Praia

Largo da
Palma

Praça
Castro
Alves

Buses for Bonfim
& Barra

Museu de Arte
Sacra de Bahia

Mosteiro de
São Bento

Tempostal

SANTA TEREZA

Palacete
das Artes &
Museu Rodin

➡ Salvador maps
1 Salvador orientation, page 21
2 Salvador centre, page 25
3 Pelourinho, page 30
4 Salvador south to Barra, page 34

Estadio
Otávio
Mangabeira

Dique
de Tororó

Largo 2
de Julho

Praça Duque
de Caxias

Praça
Piedade

Museu de Arte
Moderna

To Barra

4

Note Most of the churches and museums in the Centro Histórico prohibit the taking of pictures; even without a flash.

Praça Municipal (Tomé de Souza) and the Praça da Sé

These adjacent squares (connected by the Rua da Misericordia), link with neighbouring Terreiro de Jesus (Praça 15 de Novembro) to form an almost entirely pedestrianized zone. A decade ago this area was tawdry, but it has been tidied up in recent years. The streets are lined with stores and stalls selling arts and crafts, music and souvenirs, and there are plenty of places for snacks and refreshments.

The **Praça Municipal** is the oldest part of Salvador – where the first governor, Thomé de Souza, built the first administrative buildings and churches (after unceremoniously clearing an indigenous Tupinambá village from the site). A statue of the soldier stands on a plinth gazing wistfully out to sea at the southern end of the *praça*. From here the city grew in a bewildering panoply of architectural styles, many of which can be seen around the square. Dominating the view are the neoclassical columns of the former council chamber (1660), now the **Paço Municipal** ① *Praça Municipal s/n, T071-3176 4200, Tue-Sat 0930-1700, free*, and the imposing **Palácio Rio Branco** ① *Praça Municipal s/n, T071-3176 4200, Tue-Sat 0930-1700, free*. Like many of Brazil's opulent buildings, this was built in homage to the French for the state-governor, in 1918. The palace now houses municipal offices. On the western side of the square is the star of many postcards: the huge, art deco **Elevador Lacerda** ① *US$0.05*, which whisks people from the Cidade Alta to the Cidade Baixa, 70 m below, in seconds. It was built in the late 1920s to replace an old hydraulic lift, which in turn replaced the original rope and pulley system first installed by the Jesuits. There are wonderful views over the bay from here.

Heading north from the *praça*, Rua da Misericórdia runs past the church of **Santa Casa Misericórdia** ① *T071-3322 7666, open by arrangement 0800-1700*, (1695), with its high altar and beautiful painted *azulejos* (tiles), to **Praça da Sé**. This is one of central Salvador's most attractive squares, decorated with modernist fountains, shaded by mimosa or flamboyant trees and lined with stately buildings, many of which house smart shops or European-style cafés. Look out for the **Cruz Caída** (Fallen Cross), a sculpture of a fallen and broken crucifix by one of Latin America's foremost sculptors, Mário Cravo Junior (www.cravo.art.br). It is dedicated to the old Igreja da Sé (cathedral), which was pulled down in 1930, together with an entire street of 18th- and early 19th-century townhouses, to make way for the now defunct tramline. Some of the cathedral's foundations have been uncovered and lie bare near the Cruz, covered in wild flowers. Immediately opposite the Cruz Caída is the **Memorial da Baiana do Acarajé** ① *Praça da Sé s/n, Mon-Fri 0900-1200 and 1400-1800, US$5*, a museum and cultural centre telling the story of the *Baianas* (the Bahian women who lead the **Lavagem do Bonfim** parade and who participate in **Carnaval** throughout Brazil wearing traditional large swirling dresses). There are panels, ritual objects and historic photographs and the café next door serves Bahian snacks and has a small souvenir shop.

Terreiro de Jesus (Praça 15 de Novembro)

Immediately northeast of Praça da Sé, the Terreiro de Jesus is a large *praça* surrounded by handsome colonial townhouses and the bulk of the city's fabuous baroque churches. The square is the centre of tourist activity and bustles with bars, cafés and myriad souvenir stalls proffering everything from *acarajé* to *berimbaus*. It's particularly lively on Tuesday nights and weekends when there are shows or concerts (see Bars and clubs, page 46), and there are regular displays of **capoeira** – generally presented without joy and for the tourist dollar; if you stop to watch, you'll be expected to pay. Beware, too, of the persistent *Baianos* offering *fitas* (brightly coloured ribbons given as a good luck present), who swoop down like hawks on new arrivals. The streets that run off the south side of the Terreiro are frequented by drug dealers and beggars – best avoided, especially after dark.

The Terreiro de Jesus takes its name from the 'Church of the Society of Jesus' (ie the Jesuits) that dominates it. It is now **Catedral Basílica** ① *daily 0900-1200, 1400-1800, free*, devolving its ownership to the main body of the Catholic church in 1759, after the Jesuits were expelled from all Portuguese territories. The cathedral, whose construction dates from between 1657 and 1672, is one of the earliest examples of baroque in Brazil – a style that came to dominate in the 18th century and reached its full glory in Minas Gerais. The interior is magnificent: the vast vaulted ceiling and 12 side altars, in baroque and rococo, frame the main altar and are completely leafed in gold. This lavish display is offset by a series of Portuguese *azulejos* on in blue, white and yellow, which swirl together in a tapestry pattern.

The church is said to be built on the site of the original Jesuit chapel built by Padre Manuel da Nóbrega in the 16th century. Nóbrega was part of the crew on that came from Portugal with Brazil's first governor-general, Tomé de Sousa, arriving in Bahia on 29 March 1549. Together with Padre José de Anchieta, he founded many of the Jesuit seminaries and churches that later became the cities of modern Brazil, including Rio, Recife and São Paulo. Antônio Vieira, one of the greatest orators in Portuguese history and a campaigner for the protection of the indigenous Brazilians in the Amazon, preached some of his most famous sermons in the church. He died a sad and disgraced old man of nearly 90 in July 1697, condemned by the Dominican-run Inquisition and prohibited from either preaching or writing after being slanderously accused by his enemies of conniving in the murder of a colonial official. The cathedral also preserves the remains of Mem de Sá, the great and brutal Portuguese conquistador and third governor-general of Brazil, who perhaps more than anyone was responsible for the establishment of the Brazilian territories. He ruthlessly crushed the Tupinambá along the Bahian coast and, in liberating Rio from the French, he quelled an insurrection that threatened to overthrow the fledgling Brazilian colony. Note the interesting sculptures, particularly those on the altar of Saint Ursula in a huge chest carved from a trunk of Mata Atlântica *jacarandá*, encrusted with ivory, bone and turtle shell.

Across the square is the church of **São Pedro dos Clérigos** ① *Praca 15 de Novembro, T071-3321 9183, Mon-Fri 0900-1200 and 1400-1800, free*, which is beautifully renovated. Alongside is the church of the early 19th-century **Ordem Terceira de São Domingos** ① *Praca 15 de Novembro, T071-3242 4185, Mon-Fri 0900-1200 and 1400-1700, free*, which has a beautiful 18th-century, painted wooden ceiling attributed to José Joaquim da Rocha, the father of the Bahian School – perhaps the first Brazilian school of art to adopt the contemporaneous European trompe l'oeil style – which used perspective to create the illusion of three-dimensions.

There are two interesting museums on the square, both housed in the former Jesuit College (and subsequent Bahian School of Medicine building). The **Museu Afro-Brasileiro (MAfro)** ① *Mon-Fri 0900-1800, Sat and Sun 1000-1700, US$3 for a joint ticket with MAE*, charts the history of Africans in Bahia. Between 1440-1640, Portugal monopolized the export of slaves from Africa and they were the last European country to abolish it. Over the course of 450 years, they were responsible for transporting more than 4.5 million Africans – some 40% of the total. There are countless exhibits, from both Brazil and the African continent itself, including fascinating ritual objects, musical instruments and textiles. Panels compare West African and Bahian *orixás* (deities) and, in a gallery all to themselves, are some beautiful wooden carved effigies by the artist Carybé (Hector Julio

Candomblé

Candomblé is a spiritual tradition that developed from religions brought over by Yoruba slaves from West Africa. It is focused on relationships with primordial spirits or orixás who are linked with natural phenomena and the calendar. The orixas are invoked in terreiros (temples). These can be elaborate, decorated halls, or simply someone's front room with tiny altars. Ceremonies are divided into two distinct parts. The first is when the orixás are invoked through different rhythms, songs and dances. Once the dancers have been possessed by the orixá, they are led off in a trance-like state to be changed into sacred, often very elaborate costumes, and come back to the ceremonial area in a triumphant procession in which each one dances separately for their deity. Overseeing the proceedings are mães or pães de santo, priestesses or priests.

Candomblé ceremonies may be seen by tourists, usually on Sundays and religious holidays – although many are just for show and not the real thing. The ceremonies can be very repetitive and usually last several hours, although you are not under pressure to remain for the duration. Appropriate and modest attire should be worn; visitors should not wear shorts, sleeveless vests or T-shirts. White clothing is preferred, black should not be worn especially if it is combined with red. Men and women are separated during the ceremonies, women always on the left, men on the right. No photography or sound recording is allowed. Most temples are closed during Lent, although each one has its own calendar. **Bahiatursa** (see page 23) has information about forthcoming ceremonies, but accurate information on authentic festivals is not always easy to come by.

Páride Bernabó) who lived most of his life in Bahia. Carybé became famous with the antropofagismo movement, illustrating Mario de Andrade's Macunaíma, and won the prize as the best draughtsman in Brazil in 1955. He was later celebrated for his depictions of candomblé rituals and orixás. In the basement of the same building, the **Museu de Arqueologia e Etnologia (MAE)** ⓘ Mon-Fri 0900-18700, Sat and Sun 1000-1700, US$3 for a joint ticket with MAfro, houses indigenous Brazilian artefacts collected from all over Brazil over the centuries by the Jesuits, alongside archaeological discoveries from Bahia, such as stone tools, clay urns and rock art.

Largo Cruzeiro de São Francisco and the Franciscan churches

Facing Terreiro de Jesus is the **Largo Cruzeiro de São Francisco**, crowded with souvenir stalls and dominated by a large wooden cross and the church and the modest façade of the convent of **São Francisco** ⓘ Largo do Cruzeiro de São Francisco, T071-3322 6430, Mon-Sat 0800-1700, Sun 0800-1600, US$2. The convent is the jewel in Salvador's baroque crown and one of the finest baroque churches in Latin America. The entrance leads to a sanctuary with another spectacular trompe l'oeil painting by José Joaquim da Rocha (1777) and to a set of cloisters decorated with minutely detailed and hand-painted azulejos; many are by the celebrated Portuguese artist Bartolomeu Antunes de Jesus. Each tile is based on illustrations to epigrams by Horace by the 17th-century Flemish humanist and teacher of Peter Paul Rubens, Otto Venius. "Quem e Rico? Quem nada ambiciona", proclaims one ('Who is rich? He who is ambitious for nothing'). The picture shows a man crowned from behind by a bare-breasted woman (representing glory) whilst simultaneously pushing away golden crowns (representing the trappings of aristocracy and establishment). It's hard not to regard this as irony when entering the church itself. It took 64 years to cover the interior with plated gold and iconic art; almost all of it paid for by that same establishment who had grown wealthy on the sugar trade. The irony is compounded by more *azulejos* around the altar showing scenes from St Francis' life – which was remarkable for the saint's Siddhartha-like rejection of his aristocratic birth right, in favour of mendicancy.

Irony aside, only a resolute inverted snob could fail to be transfixed by the artistry inside church. The main body of the church is the most opulent in Brazil – a vast, ornate exuberance of woodcarving in *jacarandá* depicting a riot of angels, animals, floral designs and saints, covered with some 800 kg of solid gold. It's easy to see that the work is by Africans and native Brazilians. Look out for the mask-like faces on the top right- and left-hand corners of the sacristy – an allusion to contemporaneous African art; and the cherubs below the pulpit and encrusted into the walls, whose genitals were hacked off by Portuguese far more prudish than those who carved their church. There are wonderful individual pieces too, including a beautiful sculpture of St Peter of Alcântara (venerated for his mystical visions attained in a state of painful ecstasy), agonisingly captured by the one of the fathers of Bahian baroque sculpture, Manoel Inácio da Costa. He was born in Camamu and known as 'Seis Dedos' (six fingers) to his contemporaries. And he chipped the figure from a single hunk of rainforest wood. Other unspecified statues are known to be by Bento dos Reis, born to African slaves and celebrated for the emotion he imparts to his figures. They may include a serene statue of the patron saint of African-Brazilians, the hermit Saint Benedict, born to Ethiopian slaves in Messina in Sicily in 1524 (beatified by Pope Benedict XIV in 1743), and invited to join the Franciscans order after suffering a racist jibe. He carries the Christ child in his arms. The names of the painters of the dozens of magnificent ceiling panels remain unknown.

Next door is the church of the **Ordem Terceira de São Francisco** ① *Ladeira da Ordem Terceira de São Francisco 3, T071-3321 6968, Mon-Sat 0800-1700, Sun 0800-1600, US$2,* (1703), with an intricate sandstone façade in the Spanish Churrigueresque style – an elaborate rococo form characterized by exuberant carving. It is one of only two such churches in the country and its carvings were completely covered over with plaster until the early 20th century, probably in protest against associations with Spain. There's a huge and intricately decorated altarpiece inside, a chapterhouse covered in striking images of the Order's most celebrated saints and a series of *azulejos* many depicting scenes of Lisbon before the devastating earthquake in 1755.

The Pelourinho

The streets north of the Terreiro de Jesus, which run over a series of steep hills to the neighbourhood of Santo Antônio, are referred to as the Pelourinho. The area takes its name from the whipping post where the African slaves were auctioned off or punished by their Brazilian-Portuguese masters. Its steep cobbled streets are lined with brightly painted townhouses leading to little *praças* and always thronging with people. The bulk of the restaurants, small hotels and shops in the Centro Histórico are to be found here, and the streets are great for a browse.

The Pelourinho's main thoroughfares run north off the Terreiro de Jesus. **Rua Alfredo Brito** (aka Portas do Carmo) and **Rua João de Deus** and the side streets that run off them are lined with three- or four-storey townhouses occupied by shops, restaurants and boutique hotels. Both descend in steep cobbles to the **Largo de Pelourinho**, a large sunny

3 Pelourinho

To Forte Santo Antônio, Santo Antônio & Carmo Church

Largo Jubiabá
Lad do Passo
R Ribeiro dos Santos
Lad do Carmo
R das Flores

Conjunto do Benin
R Pe A Gomes

Nossa Senhora do Rosários dos Pretos

Av Miguel Calmon
R Cons Dantas
R Pedro A Cabral
R-to Julião

Lad do Taboão

Largo de Pelourinho

Casa da Nigéria
Oficina Musical

Fundação Casa de Jorge Amado

CIDADE ALTA
CENTRO HISTÓRICO

Museu da Cidade

R L de Carvalho

Plano Inclinado Gonçalves

Praça Quincas Berro d'Agua

Lad do Ferrão

R Gregório de Matos

Museu Abelardo Rodrigues

Museu Afro-Brasileiro & Museu do Arqueologia e Etnologia

R Portas do Carmo (Alfredo Brito)
R J C Rabelo

Cana Brava

Instituto Mauá & Tourist Information

R Frei Vicente

Catedral Basílica

Cruz Caída Monument

Largo Teresa Batista

Goya Lopes

R João de Deus

Memorial de Baiana do Acarajé

Praça da Sé

São Pedro dos Clérigos

Terreiro de Jesus (Praça 15 de Novembro)

R das Laranjeiras

Tourist Police

Bradesco

Ilê Aiyê

Santa Casa da Misericórdia

R da Misericórdia

Ordem Terceira de São Domingos

R Gregório de Matos (R Muniz Barreto)

To Lacerda Lift & Mercado Modelo

To Praça Municipal

Largo Cruzeiro de São Francisco

R do Bispo

R Três de Maio

R da Ordem Terceira

R Guedes Brito

R 28 de Setembro

Lad da Praça

R São Francisco

São Francisco

Ordem Terceira de São Francisco

R Santa Isabel

N

50 metres
50 yards

Where to stay 🛏
Albergue das Laranjeiras, Café & Creperie 4 *D3*
Albergue do Peló 6 *A3*
Albergue São Jorge 6 *B2*
Casa do Amarelindo 10 *B2*
Solar das Artes 1 *D3*
Hostel Cobreu 3 *A3*
Pelourinho 8 *B3*
Studio do Carmo 13 *A3*
Villa Bahia 12 *D2*

Restaurants 🍴
Axego 3 *C2*

Bahia Café 5 *C1*
Coffee Shop 10 *C1*
Gramado 15 *C1*
Jardim das Delícias 8 *C2*
Mão Dupla 2 *D3*
Mama Bahia 9 *B3*
Maria Mata Mouro 7 *D3*
Negro's 11 *B2*
O Nilo 13 *D3*
Senac 4 *A3*
Sorriso de Dadá 1 *C3*
Uauá 6 *B3*

Bars & clubs 🍸
Cantina da Lua 18 *C2*
Casa do Olodum 17 *C3*
Do Reggae 20 *A3*
O Cravinho 19 *C1*

square watched over by one of Salvador's most important African-Brazilian monuments, the church of **Nossa Senhora do Rosário dos Pretos** ① *Praça Jose Alencar s/n, Largo do Pelourinho, T071-3241 5781, Mon-Fri 0830-1800, Sat and Sun 0830-1500 and with African-Brazilian Mass every Tue at 1800, free*, built by former slaves over a period of 100 years, with what little financial resources they had. In colonial times, black Bahians were not even allowed to walk in front of the churches reserved for the white elite, let alone go inside them, and had to worship in their own building. The side altars honour black saints such as São Benedito (see Convento do São Francisco, above) and the painted ceiling and panels are by Jose Joaquim da Rocha. The overall effect is of simple tranquillity, in contrast to the busy opulence of the cathedral and the São Francisco church. The church remains a locus for black Bahian culture and has strong connections with *candomblé*. On Tuesdays, following a show by Olodum on the Pelourinho, there is an African-Brazilian Mass with singing accompanied by percussion from repiques, tambors and tamborins. Be sure to visit the haunting **Slave Cemetery** at the back of the building.

At the corner of Alfredo Brito and Largo do Pelourinho is a small museum dedicated to the work of Bahia's most famous author Jorge Amado, **Fundação Casa de Jorge Amado** ① *Largo do Pelourinho s/n, T071-3321 0070, www.jorgeamado.org.br, Mon-Fri 0900-1800, Sat 1000-1600, free*. Amado was born and brought up around Ilhéus but spent much of his life in this house. The people of this part of Salvador provided the inspiration for the larger-than-life characters that populate some of his most famous novels including *Dona Flor e seus dois Maridos* (*Dona Flor and Her Two Husbands*, 1966). Information is in Portuguese only, but the walls of the museum café are covered with colourful copies of his book jackets in scores of languages, and all of his work is on sale.

Next door is the **Museu da Cidade** ① *Praça Jose de Alencar 3, Largo do Pelourinho, T071-3321 1967, Tue-Fri 0900-1830, Sat 1300-1700, Sun 0900-1300, free*, in two adjacent 18th-century houses and with exhibitions of arts and crafts, old photographs of the city, many fascinating objects from *candomblé* rituals and effigies of the *orixás*. A further room is devoted to the life and ouvre of the 19th-century abolitionist Antônio Frederico de Castro Alves (1847-1871), and from the higher floors there is a good but seldom photographed view of the Pelourinho.

Just around the corner from the Largo do Pelourinho is the **Museu Abelardo Rodrigues** ① *Solar do Ferrão, R Gregório de Matos 45, T071-3320 9383, Tue-Sat 1300-1800, US$2*, which preserves one of the most important and impressive collections of religious art outside the São Paulo's Museu de Arte Sacra. It is housed in one of the Pelourinho's best-preserved and most stately 18th-century townhouses – once a Jesuit college – and showcases some impressive statuary, engravings, paintings and lavish monstrances from Brazil, all over Latin America and the Far East. All were collected by the Pernambucan who gave the museum its name. There is also a smaller and less illustrious sacred art musuem, the **Museu de Arte Sacra da Bahia** (see page 33).

Below Nossa Senhora do Rosario dos Pretos is the **Conjunto do Benin** ① *R Padre Agostinho Gomes 17, Pelourinho, T071-3241 5679, casadobenin@yahoo.com.br, Mon-Fri 1200-1800*, which has displays of African-Brazilian crafts, photos and a video on Benin and Angola. It hosts exhibitions, dance shows and other artistic events. The **Casa da Nigéria** ① *R Alfredo de Brito 26, Pelourinho, T071-3328 3782*, offers a similar programme orientated more to Yoruba culture and has showcases of African and African-Brazilian arts and crafts, photographs and an important library. Yoruba language classes are available here and both cultural centres are important nexuses of African-Brazilian culture and society in Bahia. The **Quilombo do Pelô** hotel also serves as a cultural centre for Jamaican culture.

There are occasional shows in the restaurant (where Jamaican food is served) and the hotel receives many Jamaican celebrity guests. There's also Jamaican-Brazilian fusion music played in the **Bar do Reggae** (see page 46).

Morro do Carmo and Santo Antônio

The Ladeira do Carmo climbs up the steep **Morro do Carmo** hill running north from the Largo do Pelourinho, past the **Igreja do Santissimo Sacramento do Passo** and the steps that lead up to it (which were the setting for the city scenes in Anselmo Duarte's award-winning socio-political tragedy, *O Pagador de Promessas*, 'Keeper of the Promises'), to the **Largo do Carmo**. This little *praça*, at the junction of the Ladeira do Carmo and Rua Ribeiro dos Santos, is watched over by a series of Carmelite buildings. The most impressive is the **Igreja da Ordem Terceira do Carmo** ① *Morro do Carmo s/n, Mon-Sat 0800-1130, 1400-1730, Sun 1000-1200, US$1*, once a piece of striking baroque dating from 1709 but completely gutted in a fire 67 years later and restored in the 19th century. It is in a poor state of repair but houses one of the sacred art treasures of the city, a sculpture of Christ made in 1730 by Francisco Xavier 'O Cabra' Chagas ('the Goat'), a slave who had no formal training but who is celebrated by many locals as the Bahian Aleijadinho. Two thousand tiny rubies embedded in a mixture of whale oil, ox blood and banana resin give Christ's blood a ghostly, almost transparent appearance and the statue itself so lifelike it appears almost to move. There is a small museum with a collection of ornate icons and period furniture. The adjacent **Igreja do Carmo** ① *Morro do Carmo s/n, Mon-Sat 0800-1200, 1400-1800, Sun 0800-1200, US$1*, a magnificent painted ceiling by the freed slave, José Teófilo de Jesus, while the **Convento do Carmo**, which served as a barracks for Dutch troops during the 1624 invasion, has been tastefully converted into Salvador's most luxurious hotel (see Where to stay, page 40).

Rua do Carmo continues to climb north from the Morro do Carmo into the neighbourhood of **Santo Antônio**, where dozens of the pretty colonial houses have been converted into tasteful boutique hotels and *pousadas*, the best of which have gorgeous bay views. The street eventually reaches the Barão do Triunfo (Largo de Santo Antônio), after about a kilometre. This handsome square (with barely a tourist in sight) is watched over by the hulking **Forte de Santo Antônio além do Carmo fortress** ① *Barão do Triunfo s/n, Santo Antônio, T071-3117 1488, http://fortesantoantonio.blogspot.com, Mon-Sat 0900-1200 and 1400-1700, US$4*, and another impressive church, the **Igreja de Santo Antônio Além do Carmo** ① *Largo Barão do Triunfo s/n, Santo Antônio, T071-3242 6463, Mon-Sat 0900-1200 and 1400-1730, free*. The fort dates from the last decade of the 17th century and is known locally as the Forte da Capoeira as it is home to half a dozen capoeira schools. It was restored at the turn of the 20th century and there are beautiful views over the bay from its walls.

Cidade Baixa and Mercado Modelo

Salvador's Cidade Baixa (Lower City), which sits at the base of the cliff that runs from Santo Antônio in the north to Praça Municipal and Lacerda Lift in the south, was once as delightful and buzzing with life as the Pelourinho. Today, its handsome imperial and early republican 19th-century buildings, many of them covered in *azulejos*, are crumbled and cracked. Others have been pulled down and replaced with ugly concrete warehouses. There are numerous gorgeous baroque churches in a similar state of disrepair, most of them with doors permanently closed. With the exception of the ferry docks, the whole area is dangerous and down at heel – especially at night. However, there are plans for restoration. A big hotel group has apparently bought up one of the old colonial mansions, while musician Carlinhos Brown has established the **Museu du Ritmo** ⓘ *R Torquato Bahia, 84 Edifício Mercado do Ouro, T071-3353 4333, www.carlinhosbrown.com.br/universo/museu-du-ritmo*, and the **International Centre for Black Music** – a complex built around a 1000-sq-m concert arena housed in a giant courtyard formed from the walls of a former colonial mansion house which once was home to the gold exchange. The museum has multi-media exhibits, a cinema, art gallery, school and recording studio on the site. Shows are advertized in the local press and on Carlinhos Brown's website.

There are few other sights of interest. Bahia's best souvenir shopping is in the **Mercado Modelo** ⓘ *Praça Visconde Cayru, Cidade Baixa, www.mercadomodelobahia.com.br, Wed-Mon 0900-1900, Sun 0900-1300, closed Tue*. This former customs house is thick with stalls selling everything from musical instruments to life-size sculptures hacked out of hunks of wood. Look out for the colourful handbags, made out of hundreds of can ring-pulls sewn together with fishing twine, and the *orixá* effigies and postcards. There are frequent capoeira shows between 1100 and 1300 on weekdays (you will have to pay to take pictures), occasional live music and numerous cafés and stalls selling Bahian cooking.

Further along the shore to the south is the striking, octaganol church of **Nossa Senhora da Conceição da Praia** ⓘ *R Conceição da Praia at Av Contorno*. The church, which dates from 1736, was built in *lioz* marble in Portugal by Manuel Cardoso de Saldanha, disassembled bit by bit with the stones given numbers, then transported to Salvador and reconstructed. It has an unusual octagonal nave and diagonally set towers, modelled on churches in Portugal such as the Guarda cathedral. Inside it is magnificent, with a stunning ceiling painting of an Italianate panoply of saints gathered around the Madonna in glorious Renaissance perspective – the masterpiece of José Joaquim da Rocha.

South of the centre → *For listings, see pages 40-56.*

The modern city, which is dotted with skyscraper apartment blocks, sits to the south of the old centre towards the mouth of the bay. Rua Chile leads to **Praça Castro Alves**, with its monument to the man who started the campaign that finally led to the abolition of slavery in 1888. Two streets lead out of this square: Avenida 7 de Setembro, busy with shops and street vendors selling everything imaginable; and, parallel to it, Rua Carlos Gomes. **Mosteiro São Bento** ⓘ *Av 7 de Setembro, T071-3322 4749, www.saobento.org, Mon-Fri 0900-1200 and 1300-1600, US$3*, another of Bahia's oldest religious buildings, dates from 1582 but was constructed much later. The cool, colonial spaces and cloistered garden are a welcome quiet space within the bustle of the city. The monastery was used as an arsenal by the Dutch during their occupation in 1624 and narrowly avoided going the way of much of colonial Rio and São Paulo in the 20th century, which were razed to the ground to make way for ugly modern skyscrapers. It houses a religious art museum with some 2000 priceless antiquities.

Just to the south is the **Palacete das Artes** ⓘ *R da Graça 284, Graça, T071-3117 6986, www.palacetedasartes.ba.gov.br, Tue-Sun 1000-1800, free*, a small museum and cultural centre showing temporary exhibitions from Brazilian and notable Bahian artists, who in the past have included the likes of Mario Cravo Junior.

Museu de Arte Sacra da Bahia ⓘ *R do Sodré 276 off R Carlos Gomes, T071-3243 6511, www.museudeartesacradabahia.com.br, Mon-Fri 1130-1730, US$2*, is in the 17th-century monastery and church of Santa Teresa d'Avila, at the bottom of the steep Ladeira de Santa Tereza. Many of the 400 carvings are from Europe, but there are some beautiful pieces by the artists who worked on the city's finest churches, such as Frei Agostinho de Piedade and José Joaquim da Rocha. Look out for the hauntingly life-like statue of Christ by the latter,

Where to stay 🛏

Albergue do
  Porto 11
Alpha Hostel 1
Bahia Flat 3
Ché Lagarto 8
Farrol Barra Flat 10
La Villa
  Française 9
Monte Pascoal
  Praia 5
Pousada Azul 6
Pousada Hotel
  Âmbar 7
Pousada Marcos 13
Villa Romana 15
Village Novo
  Beach Suites 16

Restaurants 🍴
Barravento 2
Caranguejo do
  Farol 4
Oceánica 5
Quattro Amicci 1

➡ **Salvador maps**
1 Salvador orientation, page 21
2 Salvador centre, page 25
3 Pelourinho, page 30
4 Salvador south to Barra, page 34

carved from a piece of ivory and crucified on a *jacarandá* cross. Among the reliquaries of silver and gold is one made from gilded wood by Aleijadinho. The views from the patio, out over the Baía de Todos os Santos, are breathtaking and very little photographed. Opposite is **Tempostal** ① *R do Sodré 276, Tue-Fri 0900-1830, Sat and Sun 0900-1800*, a private museum of postcards. Just inland near Campo Belo is the **Dique do Tororo** ① *Av Vasco de Gama*, a lake and leisure area decorated with 3-m-high *orixá* statues by the Bahian sculptor Tatti Moreno. There are large *candomblé* celebrations here at dawn on 2 February before the **Festa da Yemanjá**.

Further south, the **Museu de Arte Moderna and Solar do Unhão** ① *off Av Contorno, T071-3117 6139, www.mam.ba.gov.br, Tue-Fri 1300-1900, Sat 1300-2100, free*, is one of the finest modern art museums in northeastern Brazil. The collection includes work by most of Brazil's important artists, including Emiliano di Cavalcanti, the abstract painter Alfredo Volpi, social-expressionist Cândido Portinari and the co-founder of *antropofagismo*, Tarsila do Amaral; alongside pieces by Bahian artists such as Mario Cravo Junior, Carybé and the Franco-Bahian photographer Pierre Verger; and contemporary artists like Jose Bechara, Siron Franco and the photographer Mario Cravo Neto. The gallery is housed in the Solar do Unhão – itself an important historical monument. It sits right on the waterfront and was built in the 17th century initially as a sugar storage way station. It then became a mansion occupied by a series of influential Bahians over the following centuries, all of whom have left their mark on the building – from little chapels to beautiful painted *azulejos*. The gallery also hosts temporary exhibitions, has an arts cinema (www.saladearte.art.br) and a bar/café with live jazz on Saturdays from 1830. There are many restaurants nearby. The museum is close to a *favela* and there are occasional muggings particularly after dark; it's best to take a taxi.

Heading towards Porta da Barra, the **Museu de Arte da Bahia** ① *Av 7 de Setembro 2340, Vitória, Tue-Fri 1400-1900, Sat and Sun 1430-1900, US$2*, has interesting paintings by Bahian and Brazilian artists from the 18th to the early 20th century and a collection of 18th- and 19th-century furniture. A kilometre south of here is the **Museu Carlos Costa Pinto** ① *Av 7 de Setembro 2490, Vitória, www.museucostapinto.com.br, Mon and Wed-Fri 1430-1900, Sat and Sun 1500-1800, US$2*, in a modern house, with collections of crystal, porcelain, silver and furniture. It ostensibly has the world's only collection of *balangandãs* (slave charms and jewellery). The museum has a pleasant little garden café serving quiches, salads and cakes.

Porto da Barra and the Atlantic beach suburbs

Barra is one of the most popular places to stay in Salvador and has the best inner-city beaches. The strip from Porto da Barra as far as the Cristo at the end of the Farol da Barra beach has some of the city's liveliest cafés, restaurants, bars and clubs. A night out here, in nearby Campo Belo and in the exclusive restaurants and bars of the city's most upmarket venue, **Praça dos Tupinambas**, give an idea of how polarized Salvador society is. The clientele is much more middle class than the Pelourhino; the music, food and conversation are more European and American and, in Brazil's African heart, there's hardly a black face in sight.

There are a few sights of moderate interest around Barra. The **Forte de Santo Antônio** and its famous lighthouse are right at the mouth of the bay where Baía de Todos os Santos and the South Atlantic Ocean meet. On the upper floors of the lighthouse, the **Museu Hidrográfico** ① *Tue-Sat 1300-1800, US$2*, has fine views of the coast. A promenade leads away from the fort, along the beach to the **Morro do Cristo** at the eastern end, which is crowned with a statue of Christ, arms outstretched over the bay. The statue is unremarkable in itself, but there are good views from the hill.

Rio Vermelho and the ocean beaches

From Barra the beach road runs east through the beachfront suburbs of **Ondina** and **Rio Vermelho**. Confusingly, the road is known as both Avenida Oceânica and Avenida Presidente Vargas, and both have different numbering, making finding an address rather challenging. Rio Vermelho is the only suburb of interest. It has long been the home of many of Salvador's well-to-do artists and musicians and a centre for *candomblé*. Unlike the beachfront neighbourhoods around Barra, the clientele is a healthy mix of middle class and African-Brazilian. There's a lively market with many little spit-and-sawdust bars, a handful of decent restaurants and small eateries serving some of the city's best *acarajé*. The area is busy at night, especially at weekends, and there are a number of venues playing traditional Bahian music. On 2 February the beach at Rio Vermelho is packed with *candomblé* pilgrims for the **Festa de Yemanjá**. To get here from the city centre, it is a 10-minute taxi ride (US$10-12) or a 20-minute bus journey on the airport–city centre bus. There are some good hotels nearby.

The next beaches along from Rio Vermelho are **Amaralina** and **Pituba**, neither of which are good for swimming but both of which have good surf and small fishing communities. Look out for *jangadas* (small rafts with sails peculiar to northeast Brazil) on the seashore. Bathing is better at **Jardim de Alah**, **Jaguaripe**, **Piatã** and **Itapoã**, all of which are fairly clean and have fluffy white sand and swaying coconut palms; any bus from Praça da Sé marked 'Aeroporto' or 'Itapoã' reaches the beaches in about an hour. Near Itapoã is the **Lagoa do Abaeté**, a deep freshwater lake surrounded by brilliant white sands. This is where local women come to wash their clothes and then lay them out to dry in the sun. The road leading up from the lake offers a panoramic view of the city in the distance with white sands and freshwater less than 1 km from the sea.

Beyond Itapoã are the magnificent ocean beaches of **Stella Maris** and **Flamengo**, both quiet during the week but very busy at the weekends. Beware of strong undercurrents.

North of the centre: Bonfim, Itapagipe and Ribeira → *For listings, see pages 40-56.*

The most famous sight in the northern suburbs is the church of **Nosso Senhor do Bonfim** ① *Largo do Bomfim 236, Bonfim, T071-3316 2196, www.senhordobonfim.org.br, museum Tue-Fri 0800-1200 and 1400-1700, free; take bus S021-00 marked Ribeira-Pituba from the the parada de ônibus (bus stop) on Av da França on the quayside in the Cidade Baixa,* (1745), on the Itapagipe Peninsula. It draws extraordinary numbers of supplicants (particularly on Friday and Sunday), making ex-voto offerings to the image of the Crucified Lord set over the high altar. The processions over the water to the church on the third Sunday in January are particularly interesting. The church has some naturalistic interior paintings by Franco Velasco (the modest canvases of the Stations of the Cross) and José Teófilo de Jesus (who painted the ceiling and 34 of the canvases on the church wall). Both almost certainly learnt their techniques from the master José Joaquim da Rocha.

The beach south of the church is far too dirty for swimming and is always busy with touts offering *fita* ribbons. It is the focus for celebrations during the festival of Nosso Senhor dos Navegantes. The colonial fort of **Monte Serrat** ① *R Santa Rita Durão s/n, T071-3313 7339, Tue-Sun 0900-1700, US$0.50,* has unusual round towers. It is one of the best preserved colonial forts in northeast Brazil and was first constructed in 1583 and altered in the 18th and 19th centuries. It sits next to the pretty Portuguese church of **Nossa Senhora do Monte Serrat** on Monte Serrat – a much photographed local beauty spot overlooking the Baía de Todos os Santos and Bonfim beach.

Further north, at Ribeira, is the church of **Nossa Senhora da Penha** (1743), another beautiful colonial building and important syncretistic pilrgrimage site. The beach here has many restaurants, but is polluted.

Ilha de Itaparica and the Baía de Todos os Santos → *For listings, see* *pages 40-56. Phone code: 071.*

Salvador sits on a peninsula which forms the northern head of Brazil's largest bay, the Baía de Todos os Santos. The bay is studded with tropical islands, the largest of which, Itaparica, sits immediately opposite Salvador, forming the bay's southern head. Itaparica is the only island close to Salvador with water clean enough for swimming. It is only 29 km long and 12 km wide and can easily be visited on a day trip.

There are two tiny towns on the island and a cluster of hamlets. **Itaparica** is very picturesque and well worth a visit, with a decent beach and many fine residential buildings from the 19th century. The church of **São Lourenço** is one of the oldest in Brazil, and a stroll through the old town is delightful. In summer the streets are ablaze with the blossoms of the beautiful flamboyant trees. Itaparica town is connected to the main ferry port at **Bom Despacho** via a coastal road run by small buses and *combi* minivans via the hamlets of **Ponta de Areia** (with good beaches and many *barracas*), **Amoureiras** and **Manguinhos**. Bom Despacho itself is little more than a ferry dock shops and restaurants. Buses to and from Valença arrive and leave from here.

The island's principal town is **Mar Grande** (aka Veracruz). There are many *pousadas* and a cluster of restaurants here, as well as at the beaches of Mar Grande and **Penha**, to the south. Beaches get better and more deserted the further south you go. They include the **Barra do Gil** (backed with holiday homes), the **Barra do Pote** (with a white-sand beach and calm waters) and **Tairu** (deserted during the week and with fine, white sand).

Ilha de Itaparica

Arriving in Ilha de Itaparica and the Baía de Todos os Santos The island is connected to the mainland by bridge or boat. The main passenger ferry runs from the São Joaquim terminal in Salvador (see page 55) to **Bom Despacho** every 45 minutes 0540-2230. A one-way ticket for foot passengers during the week costs US$1, US$1.20 at weekends. A catamaran service for Bom Despacho departs twice daily, US$3. **Mar Grande** can be reached by a small ferry (*lancha*) from the Terminal Marítimo, in front of the Mercado Modelo in Salvador. Ferries leave every 45 minutes and take 20-40 minutes, US$3 return. There is a bridge on the southwest side of the island. Buses from mainland towns such as Nazaré das Farinhas, Valença and Jaguaribe (a small, picturesque colonial port), arrive at Bom Despacho.

From Bom Despacho there are many buses, *combis* and taxis to all parts of the island. There are no banks on the island. *Combis* and taxis can be rented for trips around the island but be prepared to bargain, US$40-50 for a half-day tour. ▶ *See page 53.*

Bay islands
There are dozens of other islands in the Baía de Todos os Santos. They include the **Ilha do Frades** and the **Ilha do Maré** (with Mata Atlântica forest and tiny fishing villages). These can be visited with organized tours with **Ilha Bela** or **Tatur** (see Tour operators, page 53).

Nazaré das Farinhas → *Phone code: 075 Population: 25,000.*
On the mainland, 60 km inland from Itaparica, Nazaré das Farinhas is reached across a bridge by bus from Bom Despacho. This 18th-century town is celebrated for its market, which specializes in the local ceramic figures, or *caxixis*. There is a large market in **Holy Week**, particularly on Holy Thursday and Good Friday. From here buses run to southern Bahia. About 12 km from Nazaré (taxi from Salvador US$4.25, bus at 1530) is the village of **Maragojipinha**, which specializes in making the ceramic figures.

Recôncavo Baiano → *For listings, see pages 40-56.*

The area around the bay and immediately west of Salvador (on the other side of the Baía de Todos os Santos) is known as the Recôncavo Baiano. This was one of the chief centres of sugar and tobacco cultivation in the 16th century and there is some fine colonial architecture here. Places of interest include the sleepy colonial towns of Cachoeira and São Felix, on the banks of the muddy Rio Paraguaçu, which are famous for their festivals and strong connection to *candomblé*. There are also small fishing villages on the bay that are worth exploring, and dotted throughout the countryside are the decaying ruins of once-productive *engenhos* (sugar refineries), some of which can be visited.

Santo Amaro da Purificação and around → *Phone code: 075.*
Some 73 km from Salvador, Santo Amaro da Purificação is an old and sadly decaying sugar centre. It is noted for its churches (which are often closed because of robberies), the most famous of which is the **Igreja Matriz Santo Amaro da Purificação** ① *Praça da Purificação, T075-3241 1172, Mon-Fri 0800-1200 and 1400-1700, Sat 0800-1200*, which has a superb painted ceiling by José Joaquim da Rocha. There is also a municipal palace (1769), a fine *praça* and ruined sugar baron mansions including **Araújo Pinto**, the former residence of the Barão de Cotegipe. It is also the birthplace of Caetano Veloso and his sister Maria Bethânia. Other attractions include the splendid beaches of the bay, the falls of Vitória and the grotto of **Bom Jesus dos Pobres**. There are a number of interesting festivals and craftwork is sold on the town's main bridge. There are no good hotels or restaurants but there are at least 20 buses a day from Salvador to Santo Amaro and onward buses to Cachoeira.

About 3 km beyond Santo Amaro on the BR-420, turn right onto the BA-878 for **Bom Jesus dos Pobres**, a small, traditional fishing village with a 300-year history. There is one good hotel. To get there, take a bus from Salvador's *rodoviária* (four a day, **Camurjipe**, US$3).

Cachoeira and São Felix → *Phone code: 075.*
Set deep in the heart of some of the oldest farmland in Brazil, **Cachoeira** and its twin town, São Felix, were once thriving river ports that provided a vital supply link with the farming

hinterland and Salvador to the east. The region was the centre of the sugar and tobacco booms, which played such an important role in the early wealth of the colony. The majestic *saveiro* (a gaff-rigged boat) traditionally transported this produce down the Rio Paraguaçu to Salvador across the bay. These boats can still occasionally be seen on the river. The town was twice capital of Bahia: once in 1624-1625 during the Dutch invasion, and once in 1822-1823 while Salvador was still held by the Portuguese.

With the introduction of roads and the decline of river transport and steam, the town stopped in its tracks in the early 20th century and thus maintains its special charm. As in Salvador, *candomblé* plays a very important part in town life (see box, page 28). Easy access by river from Salvador allowed the more traditional *candomblé* temples to move in times of religious repression. Cachoeira was the birthplace of Ana Néri, known as 'Mother of the Brazilians', who organized nursing services during the Paraguayan War (1865-1870).

There are a few interesting sights in Cachoeira. The **Casa da Câmara e Cadeia** ① *Praça da Aclamação, T075-3425 1018, daily 0800-1200 and 1400-1800, US$2,* (1698-1712), was, for a brief period when Cachoeira was the state capital in 1822, the seat of the governance of Bahia. Upstairs is the town hall (with stern notices saying no shorts or Havaianas allowed). Downstairs is a **Slavery Museum**, housed in the heavy walled dungeon where slaves were imprisoned behind two sets of strong bars. The dungeon has a sad and oppressive atmosphere.

The **Museu Regional de Cachoeira** ① *Praça da Aclamação 4, T075-3425 1123, Mon-Fri 0800-1200 and 1400-1700, Sat 0800-1230, book ahead, US$2,* has a collection of period furniture, sacred images and ecclesiastical items, paintings and documents relating to the history of the town. The dark mark on the walls near the staircase at the entrance show where the river reached during the 1989 flood.

The **Santa Casa de Misericórdia** (1734) was the colonial hospital and has a fine church attached. Other churches include: the 16th-century **Ajuda** chapel (now containing a fine collection of vestments) and the convent of the **Ordem Terceira do Carmo**, whose church has a heavily gilded interior; the **Igreja Matriz** ① *R Ana Nery s/n, Tue-Sat 0900-1200 and 1400-1700, Sun 0900-1200, free,* with 5-m-high *azulejos,* and a ceiling painting attributed to José Teolfilo de Jesus (who painted at the Bonfim church in Salvador; and **Nossa Senhora da Conceição do Monte**. All churches are either restored or in the process of restoration.

The **Fundação Hansen Bahia** ① *R 13 de Maio, T075-3425 1453, Tue-Fri 0900-1700, Sat and Sun 0900-1400,* has fine engravings by the German artist Karl Meinz Hansen, who was born in Hamburg and lived on the Pelourinho in Salvador during the 1950s. In a series of xylographs he documented the miserable lives of the downtrodden women who prostituted themselves for pennies. The museum itself is the former house of Ana Néri, Brazil's Florence Nightingale who nursed the injured during the Paraguayan War.

There is a strong **woodcarving** tradition in Cachoeira and many of its artists can be seen at work in their studios.

A 300-m railway bridge built by the British in the 19th century spans the Rio Paraguaçu to São Felix, where the **Danneman Cigar Factory** ① *Av Salvador Pinto 30, T075-3438 3716, 0830-1200 and 1300-1630,* can be visited to see hand-rolling in progress. A trail starting near the **Pousada do Convento** leads to some freshwater bathing pools above Cachoeira. There are beautiful views from above São Félix.

Arriving in Cachoeira and São Felix Cachoeira/São Felix are 116 km from Salvador, and 4 km from the BR-420. There are more than 20 daily buses from Salvador to Cachoeira (2½ hours). The quickest way to get back to Salvador is to take a motorbike taxi from

Cachoeira to the BR-420 and wait at the bus stop there; buses pass every 15 minutes and are up to an hour quicker because they have fewer stops than buses that leave from Cachoeira's town centre. There is a **Bradesco** bank on Praça Dr Aristides Milton 10, with a Visa ATM.

Cachoeira has a **tourist office** ① *R Ana Néri 4, T075-3425 1123.* It is hard to get lost as there are only a handful of streets, all spreading out from the river. The centre of the city and best point for orientation is the Praça da Aclamação and the Igreja da Ordem Terceira do Carmo.

Excursions from Cachoeira

About 6 km from Cachoeira, on the higher ground of the Planalto Baiano, is the small town of **Belém** (the turning is at Km 2.5 on the road to Santo Amaro), which has a healthy climate and is a popular place for summer homes. **Maragojipe**, a tobacco exporting port with a population of 39,000, is 22 km southeast of Cachoeira along a dirt road (BA-123); it can also be reached by boat from Salvador. If you visit, look out for the old houses and the church of São Bartolomeu, with its museum. The main festival is **São Bartolomeu**, in August. Good ceramic craftwork is sold in the town. The tobacco centre of **Cruz das Almas** can also be visited, although transport is poor.

Salvador and the Recôncavo listings

For hotel and restaurant price codes and other relevant information, see pages 8-11.

☺ Where to stay

Salvador *p20, maps p21, p25, p30 and p34*
The Centro Histórico is the ideal place to stay. The Pelourinho is best if you're on a tight budget. Santo Antônio has reasonably priced hotels with charm and character. Barra also has some reasonable options; especially for apartments with kitchens, and it lies on the seafront. Business visitors will find good services and hotels in Rio Vermelho, overlooking the ocean and a 10-min taxi ride from the centre or airport.

Accommodation in the city tends to get very full over Carnaval and New Year, when prices go up. During Carnaval it is a good idea to rent a flat. The tourist office has a list of estate agents for flat rental (eg José Mendez, T071-3237 1394/6) or you can find flats through **Paradise Properties**, www.pp-bahia.com, **Bahia Online**, www.bahia-online.net, or **Bahia Land**, T071-8133 1441, williamwisden@gmail.com. Houses or rooms can be rented from **Pierre Marbacher**, R Carlos Coqueijo 68A, Itapoã,

T071-3249 5754 (Caixa Postal 7458, 41600 Salvador), who is Swiss, owns a beach bar at Rua K and speaks English. Prices for the mid- and upper-end hotels are usually considerably cheaper when booked in advance through online travel agencies (OTAs) such as www.hotels.com and www.venere.com.

The Pelourinho *p29, map p30*
$$$$ Casa do Amerelindo, R das Portas do Carmo 6, T071-3266 8550, www.casado amarelindo.com. This refurbished colonial house offers a handful of well-appointed, modern a/c rooms, all with wooden floors and plain white walls decorated with local handicrafts. Those on the coastal side of the hotel have 2-m-tall shutter windows which open onto a sweeping view of the bay.
$$$$ Hotel Villa Bahia, Largo do Cruzeiro de São Francisco 16-18, T071-3322 4271, www.en.lavillabahia.com. This boutique hotel, part of the French **Voyeur** group, is housed in a renovated 18th-century townhouse right next to the the Convento de São Francisco. There's a little mosaic pool out back and a hot tub on the roof.
$$$$ O Convento do Carmo, R do Carmo 1, T071-3327 8400, www.pestana.com. Far

and away the best in the city and the best historical hotel in the whole of Brazil, with a range of suites in a beautifully converted baroque convent. Facilities include an excellent restaurant and spa, a small swimming pool and business services.

$$$ Bahia Café, (see Restaurants, page 45). Praça Da Sé 22, T071-3322 1266, www.bahiacafehotel.com. This intimate little European-Brazilian boutique hotel is in a great location, 2 mins' walk from the Terreiro de Jesus and the Lacerda Lift. Rooms are rustic chic with chunky beds and brightly coloured counterpanes, but little furniture. Those at the front of the building sit over the street and can be noisy. Breakfasts are ample and there is an internet café serving great coffee on the ground floor.

$$$ Hotel Pelourinho, R Alfredo Brito 20, T071-3243 2324, www.hotelpelourinho. com. A newly refurbished 1960s hotel with bright tiled and white-walled a/c en suites. The bathrooms have marble basins and glass shower cubicles and a few offer great views out over the Baía de Todos os Santos.

$$$ Studio do Carmo, Ladeira do Carmo 17, T071-3326 2426, www.studiodocarmo. com. All rooms are large, decked out in wood and white paint and splashed with colour from bed linen and local art. The best are on the top floor and have terraces.

$$$-$$ Solar das Artes, R das Laranjeiras 34, T3481 0085, www.solardasartes.net. A lovely colonial house with a range of very simple wood-floor rooms (furnished with inelegant and ill-matched 1970s and 1980s fittings). The quietest are at the back. Some have very good views.

$$ Albergue das Laranjeiras, R Inácio Accioli 13, T071-3321 1366, www. laranjeiras hostel.com.br. A big and brash HI hostel with a range of white-wall and tile-floor dorms and pricey doubles and triples in a colonial building in the heart of the historic centre. The breakfast area doubles up as a café and crêperie. English spoken and a full range of hostel services.

The hostel can be noisy but is a good for meeting other travellers.

$$ Albergue do Peló, R Ribeiro dos Santos 5, T071-3242 8061, www.alberguedopelo. com.br. A bright reception area leads to simple but freshly painted and slate-floored dorms for 4-12, with beds at the bottom end of the price range. Dormitory floors are single sex and, despite the privileged central location, the crowd is quieter than most of the larger party-orientated hostels nearby. Breakfast included.

$$ Hostel Cobreu, Ladeira do Carmo 22, T071-3117 1401, www.hostelcobreu. com. This good-value, US-run hostel is well located 2 mins from the Pelourinho, meaning that lively nightlife is literally on the doorstep (the hostel balcony overlooks a popular hangout). Rooms can therefore be very noisy on a Tue or weekend nights. Rooms and dorms are simpl. Bring your own padlock for the lockers.

$$ Hostel Nega Maluca, R Dos Marchantes 15, Santo Antônio, T071-3242 9249, www. negamaluca.com. This popular party hostel is less than 400 m from one of Pelourinho's biggest Tue night shows. It has well-maintained but small rooms and dorms with thoughtful extras like a personal bed light and mains socket for each berth. The TV common room comes with complimentary hookahs, a cat and a dog and there's a terrace slung with hammocks.

$ Albergue São Jorge, R Alfredo de Brito, T071-3266 7092, www.saojorgehostel. com. This is one of the cheapest hostels in Salvador, offering bright but small single-sex dorms, and a few doubles and triples which, unusually for a hostel, work out at only a little more expensive per person. Internet access and Wi-Fi (in the lobby) come free as does breakfast.

Santo Antônio p32
Santo Antônio is a quiet district just 5 mins' walk northeast of Pelourinho, beginning immediately after the Largo do Carmo. In

recent years it has been a popular place for Europeans to open up carefully designed *pousadas* in beautifully restored buildings. A number have magnificent views of the bay. Most are mid-range, but there are a handful of cheaper options too.

$$$$ Pousada Santo Antônio, R Direita de Santo Antônio 130, T071-3326 1270, www.hotel-santoantonio.com. Very stylish, bright and comfortable converted colonial townhouse, the best rooms have magnificent views out over the bay from your bed.

$$$ Pousada do Boqueirão, R Direita do Santo Antônio 48, T071-3241 2262, www.pousadaboqueirao.com.br. The most stylish of all the *pousadas* in Salvador. Lovingly renovated by the Italian interior designer owner and her brother – a former merchant seaman. There are a variety of themed rooms; the best at the top of the building, with wonderful views out over the Baía de Todos os Santos. Service and breakfast are excellent. Several languages spoken.

$$$ Pousada do Pilar, R Direita do Santo Antônio 24, T071-3241 6278, www.pousada dopilar.com. The a/c rooms are large, modern, decked out in raw wood and light plaster and have verandas with those excellent Baía de Todos os Santos views.

$$$ Pousada Redfish, Ladeira do Boqueirão 1, T071-3243 8473, www.hotel redfish.com. This English-owned stylish, lime-green boutique has plain, large rooms, some with terraces and open-air showers.

$$$ Pousada Villa Carmo, R do Carmo 58, T071-3241 3924, www.pousadavillacarmo. com.br. The simple but elegant a/c and fan-cooled rooms in this *pousadas* come with beautiful bay views. Look at several as some are a little cramped.

Porto da Barra and the Atlantic beach suburbs *p35*

Barra is the most popular tourist neighbourhood close to the the historic centre and, whilst the sea is none too clean

Barra, has has plenty of restaurants, beach bars and nightlife.

$$$ Bahia Flat, Av Oceânica 235, T071-3339 4140, www.bahiaflat.com.br. A range of flats, the best of which have sea views. Rooms are tastefully decorated and newly refurbished with Miró prints on the walls, patent leather sofas, glass coffee tables, large fridges, sound system and expansive mirror-fronted wardrobes. The hotel has a pool and sauna and internet.

$$$ Monte Pascoal Praia, Av Oceânica 176, Farol beach, T071-2103 4000, www.monte pascoalpraiahotel.com.br. A recently renovated 1970s hotel with simple rooms in tile and white paint, the best of which have views out over the bay.

$$ Farol Barra Flat, Av Oceanica 409, T071-3339 0000, www.farolbarraflat.com.br. More than 100 simple yet well-kept apartments with kitchenettes; all with microwaves, TVs and the best with sweeping ocean views. The best are the VIP suites – more spacious and on the top floors.

$$ Pousada Azul, R Doutor Praguer Fróes 102, T071-3011 9798, www.pousadaazul. com.br. A quiet, brilliant blue *pousada* in a semi-residential street. A handful of spartan a/c rooms decorated in white with splashes of colour from modern art, linen and curtains and wooden floors. All are furnished with solid hardwood beds and commodes. The hotel has free Wi-Fi and offers a generous breakfast.

$$ Pousada Hotel Âmbar, R Afonso Celso 485, T071-3264 6956, www.ambarpousada. com.br. A French-owned *pousada* with very simple, small fan-cooled rooms gathered around a colourful little courtyard. The management practises ecotourism by contributing to the *criança familia* social project, recycling waste and conserving water.

$$ Village Novo Beach suites, Av 7 de Setembro 3659, T071-3267 4362, www. villagenovo.com. A 125-year-old converted townhouse with a range of tastefully decorated mock-boutique hotel rooms with terraces, a large roof patio and a pleasant little café restaurant. Look at several – some are far better than others. Many of those with a beach view are obscured by trees. The hotel has an internet café in the basement.

$$ Villa Romana, R Lemos Brito 14, T071-3264 6522, www.villaromana.com.br. Simple a/c rooms with wooden floors, desks, wardrobes and en suites and formal public areas decked out with mock 18th-century furnishings. There is a small patio with a pool behind the main building.

$ Albergue do Porto, R Barão de Sergy 197, T071-3264 6600, www.alberguedoporto.com.br. This HI hostel, in a turn-of-the- 20th-century house, has spacious high-ceilinged fan-cooled and a/c rooms with wooden floors (some with en suites and baths), a comfortable communal area and good breakfasts.

$ Alpha Hostel, R Eduardo Diniz Gonçalves 128, T071-3237 6282, www.alphahostel.com. The Salvador branch of this popular Rio hostel is tucked away on a small street a block from the beach and close to bus routes on Av 7 de Setembro. Rooms and dorms are bright and colourful, but are fan-cooled only and can be stuffy – especially in the hotter months. Be wary along the backstreets in the area late at night.

$ Hostel Che Lagarto Barra, Av Oceânica 84B, T071-3235 2404, www.chelagarto.com. The Salvador branch of a busy South American party hostel chain sits in a big house less than 50 m from the beach and ideally positioned for the carnival parade. Dorms and doubles are spacious and bright, but they can be very noisy.

$ La Villa Française, R Recife 222, Jardim Brasil, T071-3245 6008, www.lavilafrancaise.com. A/c rooms are well tended, spruce and clean, and painted in bright lilacs, lemon yellows and eggshell blues. The helpful and knowledgeable French-Brazilian owners offer a sumptuous breakfast of pastries, fruit and cakes.

$ Pousada Marcos, Av Oceânica 281, T071-3264 5117, www.pousadamarcos.com.br. A simple hostel-style guesthouse in a good location near the lighthouse. Always busy.

Rio Vermelho *p36, map 21*

$$$$ Pestana Bahia, R Fonte de Boi 216, T071-3453 8000, www.pestanahotels.com.br. Newly revamped tower with wonderful views out over the ocean but no access to the beach. Pool, gym, restaurant, sauna and very good business facilities. Online discounts available. With restaurant and bar.

$$$$ Zank, Av Almirante Barroso 161, Rio Vermelho, T071-3083 4000, www.zankhotel.com.br. This discreetly designed, expensive boutique hotel sits in a converted belle-époque house 5 mins' taxi ride from Rio Vermelho's bars and restaurants. Some rooms (notably No 10) have ocean views.

$$$ Catharina Paraguaçu, R João Gomes 128, Rio Vermelho, T071-3334 0089, www.hotelcatharinaparaguacu.com.br. Small colonial-style hotel with attractive courtyards and a range of decent rooms, some of which are distinctly better than others – look carefully and, if booking online, avoid the rooms close to the street. Very good service. Recommended.

$$ Ibis, R Fonte do Boi 215, T071-3330 8300, www.accorhotels.com.br. A vast, anonymous blocky hotel in this budget business chain, with functional rooms, some of which have sea views from the upper floors. Wi-Fi access throughout.

Ilha de Itaparica *p37*

$$ Galeria Hotel, Praia do Sol, Barra Grande, T071-3636 8441, www.galeria-hotel.com. German/Brazilian-owned *pousada* with simple tile-floored a/c en suites around a large pool and a good restaurant.

$$ Pousada Arco Iris, Estrada da Gamboa 102, Mar Grande beach, T071-3633 1130, www.pousadadoarcoiris.com. Magnificent though dishevelled 19th-century building romantically set in a garden of mango trees.

$$ Pousada Canto do Mar, Av Beira Mar s/n, Praia de Aratuba, T071-3638 2244, www.pousadaumcantodomar.com.br. Brightly coloured, simple *cabañas* set in a pretty garden overlooking what is a lively beach in summer and a quiet beach the rest of the year. Friendly staff, decent breakfast.

Cachoeira *p38*
$$ Pousada do Convento de Cachoeira, R Praça da Aclamação s/n, T075-3425 1716, www.pousadadoconvento.com.br. Refurbished rooms in a historic building in the centre of the town. The best are on the upper floor overlooking a grassy courtyard and have high wooden ceilings and chunky, handsome furniture. Those on the ground floor are simpler in whitewash and tile and some are only fan-cooled.
$ Pousada d'Ajuda, R Largo d'Ajuda s/n, T075-3425 5278. Spacious and clean doubles with little corners cordoned off for showers (ask to see a few rooms, some have saggy mattresses) and dorms for up to 4. Right next to the Igreja da Boa Morte.
$ Pousada La Barca, R Inocência Boaventura 37, 200 m downstream of the Praça Aclamação, T075-3425 1070, www. labarca.zip.net. Little rooms in a bright orange annexe and public areas decorated with the paintings by the artist owner Cristina. No a/c.

❼ Restaurants

The Pelourinho *p29, map p30*
$$$ Maria Mata Mouro, R da Ordem Terceira 8, T071-3321 3929. International menu, excellent service, relaxing atmosphere in a quiet corner in the bustling Pelourinho.
$$$ O Nilo, R das Laranjeiras 44, T071-9159 0937. Superior Lebanese food in an intimate little restaurant decorated with black and white prints. Great tagines and a vegetarian degustation menu.

$$$ Sorriso de Dadá, R Frei Vicente 5, T071-3321 9642, www.dada.com.br. Bahia's most famous chef has cooked for, amongst others, Michael Palin, Jorge Amado, Gilberto Gil and Hillary Clinton. Her *moqueca de camarão* and her *vatapas* are signature dishes. When Dada is at the stove all is well, when she's not, the food is now very patchy and can be expensive.
$$$ Uauá, R Gregorio de Matos, 36, T071-3321 3089. Elegant, colonial restaurant and bar serving northeastern cooking and seafood, including some Bahian specialities. The restaurant's name means 'firefly' in Tupi.
$$$-$$ Al Carmo, R do Carmo 66, Santo Antônio, T071-3242 0283. A favourite spot to watch the sun sink over the Baía de Todos os Santos, caipirinha or chilled wine in hand. The Italian food is rather stodgy and heavy with cheese. Opt for a starter only. The music (usually a guitarist and singer) has an optional cover charge.
$$$-$$ Axego, R João de Deus 1, T071-3242 7481. An established restaurant celebrated for its seafood. The *moquecas* are perhaps the best in the Centro Histórico and there is excellent *feijoada* on Sun lunchtime. Meals are served in a pleasant upstairs dining room. In a great location less than a 1-min walk from the Terreiro de Jesus.
$$$-$$ Jardim das Delícias, R João de Deus, 12, T071-3321 1449. An award-winning, elegant restaurant and antiques shop set in a pretty tropical garden serving Bahian and international food accompanied by live classical or acoustic music. Very good value for its quality.
$$ Mama Bahia, R Portas do Carmo 21, T071-3322 4397. Bahian and pan-Brazilian seafood served on white table cloths by waiters in bow ties and suits. Popular dishes include *camarão tropical* (cooked in pineapple skin and served gratinada in a tangy sauce). Live acoustic music most nights.
$$ Mão Dupla, R Santa Isabel 10, T071-9916 0217. On a quiet side street off

Bahian cuisine

Bahian cooking is spiced and peppery. The main dish is *moqueca* – seafood cooked in a sauce made from coconut milk, tomatoes, red and green peppers, fresh coriander and *dendê* (palm oil). It is traditionally cooked in a wok-like earthenware dish and served piping hot at the table. *Moqueca* is often accompanied by *farofa* (manioc flour) and a hot pepper sauce which you add at your discretion – it's very mild by British or Asian standards. The *dendê* is somewhat heavy and those with delicate stomachs are advised to try the *ensopado*, a sauce with the same ingredients as the *moqueca*, but without the palm oil.

Nearly every street corner has a Bahiana selling a wide variety of local snacks, the most famous of which is the *acarajé*, a kidney bean dumpling fried in palm oil, which has its origins in West Africa. To this the *Bahiana* adds *vatapá*, a dried shrimp and coconut milk paté (also delicious on its own), *pimenta* (hot sauce) and fresh salad. For those who prefer not to eat the palm oil, the *abará* is a good substitute. *Abará* is steamed and wrapped in banana leaves.

Bahians usually eat *acarajé* or *abará* with a chilled beer on the way home from work or the beach at sunset. Another popular dish with African origins is *xin-xin de galinha*, chicken on the bone cooked in *dendê*, with dried shrimp, garlic and squash.

Recommended *Bahianas* are: **Chica**, at Ondina beach (in the street behind the Bahia Praia Hotel); **Dinha**, in Rio Vermelho (serves *acarajé* until midnight, extremely popular); **Regina** at Largo da Santana (very lively in the late afternoon); and **Cira** in Largo da Mariquita. Seek local advice on which are the most hygienic stalls to eat from.

bustling R das Laranjeiras. Chef Sandra serves great-value traditional northeastern and Bahian dishes from *bobó do camarão* to myriad *moquecas* in portions big enough for 2. Veggie options also available. Nice atmosphere.

$$ Negro's, R do Asoginho 6, T071-8812 4527. Dona Luciana who, like other Bahian chefs such as Dada has transferred her skills from her home kitchen to this simple street-side restaurant, cooks up a great *moqueca do peixe* and *escondidinho do camarão*. Tables are plastic and on the street, and there's always an interesting mix of locals and tourists dining or drinking ice-cold beer.

$$ Senac, Praça José Alencar 13-15, Largo do Pelourinho, T071-3324 4557. A catering school with 2 restaurants. Upstairs is typical Bahian cooking; downstairs is per kilo and open only for lunch; both are a/c. Dishes are better upstairs but there is plenty of choice in the buffet and options for vegetarians.

$ Bahia Café, Praça da Sé, 20, T071-3322 1266. Smart, Belgian-run internet café with good coffee, a European-style breakfast menu and decent snacks.

$ Coffee Shop, Praça da Sé 5, T071-3322 7817. Cuban-style café serving sandwiches. Excellent coffee and tea served in china cups. Doubles as a cigar shop.

$ Gramado, Praça da Sé 16, T071-3322 1727. Lunch only. The best of the few per kilo restaurants in the area. Scrupulously clean and with a reasonable choice.

Porto da Barra and the Atlantic beach suburbs *p35*

There are many a/c restaurants from cheap to medium-priced in Shopping Barra and the Barra Center Shopping.

$$$ Amado, Av Lafayete Coutinho 660, Comércio, T071-3322 3520, www.amado bahia.com.br. The best of Salvador's top-end restaurants on the Baía de Todos os Santos waterfront. The space is beautiful, set on a deck overlooking the lapping aquamarine of the Baía de Todos os Santos. The haute cuisine *moquecas* are excellent.

$$$ Barravento, Av Oceanica 814, T071-3247 2577. Very popular beach bar restaurant and hang-out with a marquee roof. Decent cocktails, *chope* and a menu of seafood, *moquecas* and steaks.

$$$ SoHo, Av Contorno 1010, Bahia Marina, T071-3322 4554. The restaurant's long bar is where Salvador's 'A-list' drink their caipirinhas. Great sushi and sashimi combinations from Paulistano chef Marcio Fushimi are served in the chic glass-walled dining room and at the open-air veranda tables overlooking the ocean.

$$ Oceánica, Presidente Vargas 1, T071-3264 3561. Open until late, especially on weekends. A long-established popular Bahian seafood restaurant.

$$ Quatro Amicci, R Dom Marcos Teixeira 35. Excellent wood-fired oven pizzas served in a bright modern space in a converted 19th-century house. Lively weekend crowd.

$ Caranguejo do Farol, Av Oceánica 235, T071-3264 7061. A buzzing bar and seafood restaurant serving great Bahian food in *refeição* portions large enough for 2. Cheap bottled beer. Strong caipirinhas.

Rio Vermelho and other neighbourhoods *p36*

$$$ Paraiso Tropical, R Edgar Loureiro, 98-B, Resgate, Cabula, www.restauranteparaiso tropical.com.br. It's a long taxi ride from Barra or the historical centre, but there is no better Bahian restaurant in Salvador. Beto Pimentel's inventive Bahian cooking has earned him accolades from the Commanderie Des Cordons Bleus De France and *Veja* magazine's restaurant critics. Dishes are contemporary takes on Bahian and northeastern Brazilian cooking, made with organic ingredients grown in the kitchen garden. And Beto himself is a colourful character with an equally colourful life story.

$$ Casa da Dinha, R João Gomes 25, Rio Vermelho, just west of the **Catharina**

Paraguaçu Hotel and a few yards from the Largo de Santana, T071-3333 0525. One of the best mid-range Bahian restaurants in the city with a varied menu peppered with Bahian specialities, steaks, fish and standard international options like pasta.

Ilha de Itaparica *p37*

There are many Bahianas selling *acarajé* in the late afternoon and early evening, in the main *praça* and by the pier at Mar Grande.

$$$ Philippe's Bar and Restaurant, Largo de São Bento, Mar Grande. The best restaurant on the island with delicious fish dishes cooked by the French owner.

$$ Volta ao Mundo, Largo de São Bento 165, Mar Grande, T071-3633 1031. A good-value buffet restaurant with a fixed price, all-you-can-eat lunchtime menu.

🎵 Bars and clubs

Centro Histórico *p23, map p25*
Nightlife is concentrated on and around the **Pelourinho** and the **Terreiro de Jesus**, where there is always a free live street band on Tue and at weekends. The Pelourinho area is also a good place to browse the bars, but be wary after 2300. There are many bars on the **Largo de Quincas Berro d'Água**, and along R Alfredo do Brito. R João de Deus and its environs are dotted with simple pavement bars with plastic tables.

The most famous music from Salvador is the *batucada* of drum orchestras like **Olodum** and **Ilê Aiyê**, whose impressive sound can be heard frequently around the Pelourinho (Olodum played on Paul Simon's *Rhythm of the Saints* album). Both groups have their own venues and play in the individual parades or *blocos* at Carnaval. **Bar do Reggae** and **Praça do Reggae**, Ladeiro do Pelourinho, by the Nossa Senhora dos Rosarios dos Pretos church. Live reggae bands every Tue and more frequently closer to Carnaval. Currently closed for renovation. Due to re-open late 2014.

Bahia's musicians recommend

Mariene de Castro is one of Brazil's most exciting new samba acts. Her debut CD *Abre Caminho* won several of Brazil's top music awards in 2007. She told *Footprint* where to go out in Salvador: "The best and most exciting music in Bahia has its roots firmly in the samba tradition. Some of the best artists are members of the Santo de Casa cultural movement who play in the Praça Pedro Arcanjo near the Pelourinho and the Espaço Cultural Barroquinha, Praça da Barroquinha, (1 km south of the Pelourinho), T061-3334 7350."

Carlinhos Brown is one of Brazil's greatest percussionists and the founder of the Timbalada drum troupe. He is one of the icons of Bahian music and a star of Carnaval. We asked him where to go to hear live music in Salvador: "At our community centre here in Candeal you can hear my band Timbalada as well as great new acts like Candombless and Beat Gabot and in the new African music centre." To get there, take a taxi to Candeal for 1800 on a Sunday and ask for 'A Casa de Carlinhos Brown'.

Cantina da Lua, Praça Quinze de Novembro 2, Terreiro De Jesus, T071-3322 4041. Open daily. Popular spot on the square with outdoor seating, but gets crowded and the food isn't great.

Casa do Ilê Aiyê, R das Laranjeiras 16, T071-3321 4193, www.ileaiye.org.br. Ilê Aiyê's headquarters and shop, where you can find information about their shows and Carnaval events.

Casa do Olodum, R Gregório de Matos 22, T071-3321 5010, www2.uol.com.br/olodum. Olodum's headquarters where they perform live every Tue and Sun at 1900 to packed crowds.

O Cravinho, Praça 15 de Novembro 3, T071-3322 6759. Dark little bar with occasional live music. Always busy. Greasy bar food is served at tree-trunk tables, usually accompanied by plentiful *cachaça*, which is made here and stored in barrels behind the bar. Be careful in this area after 2300.

Porto da Barra and the Atlantic beach suburbs *p35*

Barra nightlife is concentrated around the Farol da Barra (lighthouse) and R Marquês de Leão, which is busy with pavement bars. Like the Pelourinho the whole area is good for a browse, but be wary of pickpockets.

Bahia Café Aflitos, Largo dos Afiltos, s/n, Mirante dos Aflitos, T071-3329 0944, www.bahiacafe.com.br. The best bar views in Salvador. Come for sunset and sip a caipirinha with the Baía de Todos os Santos at your feet, or after hours to dance to international club music.

Café Cancun, Shopping Aeroclube Plaza Show. Open weekends. American-style restaurant and after-hours club with local and international DJs and European and American dance music.

Club Dolce, R Anizio Teixeira161 (Shopping Boulevard 161), Itaigara, T071-3353 5334, facebook: dolce nightclub. Open weekends. Mock-London retro nightclub in a huge shopping centre attracting a 20-something wealthy middle-class crowd. Music ranges from *axé*, *sertanejo* and *forró*, to international retro pop and club music.

Club Ego, Pestana Rio Vermelho, R Fonte do Boi 216, T071-3017 3111, www.clubego.com.br. Open weekends. The latest and currently most fashionable light on the Salvador club music scene with the best of the national and international DJs and a middle-class crowd. International dance music only. Nothing Brazilian.

Concha Acústica, Teatro Castro Alves, Praça 2 de Julho, Campo Grande, T071-3339 8000, www.tca.ba.gov.br. The city's premier small

Carnaval in Bahia

Carnival in Bahia is the largest in the world and encourages active participation. It is said that there are 1.5 million people dancing on the streets at any one time.

The **pre-carnival festive season** begins with São Nicodemo de Cachimbo (penultimate Sunday of November), followed by Santa Bárbara (4 December), then the Festa da Conceição da Praia, centred on the church of that name (open 0700-1130) at the base of the Lacerda lift. The last night is 8 December (not for those who don't like crowds!). The Festa da Boa Viagem takes place in the last week of December, in the lower city; the beach will be packed all night on 31 December. The new year kicks off on 1 January with a beautiful boat procession of Nosso Senhor dos Navegantes from Conceição da Praia to the church of Boa Viagem, on the beach of that name in the lower city. The leading boat, which carries the image of Christ and the archbishop, was built in 1892. You can follow in a sailing boat for about US$1; go early (0900) to the dock by the Mercado Modelo. A later festival is São Lázaro on the last Sunday in January.

Carnaval itself officially starts on Thursday night at 2000 when the keys of the city are given to the Carnaval King 'Rei Momo'. The unofficial opening though is on Wednesday with the Lavagem do Porto da Barra, when throngs of people dance on the beach. Later on in the evening is the Baile dos Atrizes, starting at around 2300 and going on until dawn, very bohemian, good fun. Check with **Bahiatursa** for details on venue and time (also see under Rio for Carnaval dates).

There are two distinct musical formats. The **afro blocos** are large drum-based troupes (some with up to 200 drummers) who play on the streets, accompanied by singers atop mobile sound trucks. The first of these groups was the Filhos de Gandhy (founded in 1949), whose participation is one of the highlights of Carnaval. Their 6000 members dance through the streets on the Sunday and Tuesday of Carnaval dressed in their traditional costumes, a river of white and blue in an ocean of multi-coloured carnival revellers. The best known of the recent *afro blocos* are Ilê Aiye, Olodum, Muzenza and Malê Debalê. They all operate throughout the year in cultural, social and political areas. Not all of them are receptive to foreigners among their numbers for Carnaval. The basis of the rhythm is the enormous *surdo* (deaf) drum with its *bumbum bumbum bum* anchorbeat, while the smaller repique, played with light twigs, provides a crack-like overlay. Ilê Aiye take to the streets around 2100 on Saturday night and their departure from their headquarters at Ladeira do Curuzu in the Liberdade district is not to be missed. The best way to get there is to take a taxi to Curuzu via Largo do Tanque, thereby avoiding

concert venue with quality national and international acts such as Tom Zé and Naná Vasconcelos.

Lotus, Av Almirante Marques de Leão, T071-3264 6787. Salvador's branch of the famous New York and São Paulo club. Populated with a surprisingly eclectic crowd from blue collar to fashionable upper-middle class, dancing to old-hat European and US club sounds, house and hip hop.

Madrre, Av Otávio Mangabeira 2471, Armação, T071-3346 0012. Open weekends. Salvador's most popular dance club playing international house, electro and hip hop. An eclectic but mostly middle-class crowd.

traffic jams. The ride is a little longer but much quicker. A good landmark is the Paes Mendonça supermarket on the corner of the street, from where the bloco leaves. From there it's a short walk to the departure point.

The enormous **trios eléctricos**, 12-m sound trucks with powerful sound systems that defy most decibel counters, are the second format. These trucks, each with its town band of up to 10 musicians, play songs influenced by the *afro blocos* and move at a snail's pace through the streets, drawing huge crowds. Each *afro bloco* and *bloco de trio* has its own costume and its own security personnel, who cordon off the area around the sound truck. The *bloco* members can thus dance in comfort and safety.

The traditional Carnaval route is from Campo Grande (by the Tropical Hotel da Bahia) to Praça Castro Alves near the old town. The *blocos* go along Avenida 7 de Setembro and return to Campo Grande via the parallel Rua Carlos Gomes. Many of the trios no longer go through the Praça Castro Alves, once the epicentre of Carnaval. The best night at Praça Castro Alves is Tuesday (the last night of Carnaval), when the famous 'Encontro dos Trios' (Meeting of the Trios) takes place. *Trios* jostle for position in the square and play in rotation until the dawn on Ash Wednesday. It is not uncommon for major stars from the

Bahian (and Brazilian) music world to make surprise appearances.

There are grandstand seats at Campo Grande throughout the event. Day tickets for these are available the week leading up to Carnaval. Check with Bahiatursa for information on where the tickets are sold. Tickets are US$10 (or up to US$30 on the black market on the day). The *blocos* are judged as they pass the grandstand and are at their most frenetic at this point. There is little or no shade from the sun so bring a hat and lots of water. Best days are Sunday to Tuesday. For those wishing to go it alone, just find a friendly *barraca* in the shade and watch the *blocos* go by. Avoid the Largo da Piedade and Relógio de São Pedro on Avenida 7 de Setembro: the street narrows here, creating human traffic jams.

The other major centre for Carnaval is Barra to Ondina. The **blocos alternativos** ply this route. These are nearly always *trios eléctricos*, connected with the more traditional *blocos* who have expanded to this now very popular district. Not to be missed here is Timbalada, the drumming group formed by the internationally renowned percussionist Carlinhos Brown.

Ticket prices range from US$180 to US$450. The quality of the *bloco* often depends on the act that plays on the *trio*. For more information see the official Carnaval site, www.carnaval. salvador.ba.gov.br.

Rio Vermelho *p36*

The district of **Rio Vermelho** was once the bohemian section of town and it still has good live music and exciting bar nightlife. There are a number of lively bars around the **Largo de Santana**, a block west of Hotel Catharina Paraguaçu. The *bairro* as a whole is well worth exploring on a bar crawl Thu-Sun.

Casa da Mãe, R Guedes Cabral 81, T071-3334 3041 or T071-9601 6616 (mob), www.eventoscasadamae.blogspot.com.br. Live *samba de roda* several times a week and roots Bahian music. Ring ahead to find out the schedule.

Havana Music Bar, R Cardeal da Silva 117, T071-3237 5107. Live bands (mostly rock) Wed-Sat. Best after 2230.

Why I love carnival in Bahia

"I love that Carnival in Salvador is so huge (some 3 million people) and so diverse. We have the popular fun of *axé* music, samba and other styles, alongside Brazil's African heritage, with the *afoxés* – some of which were founded in the first half of the 20th century – and the Afro *blocos*.

Don't miss the parade by our oldest Afro *bloco*, Ilê Aiyê (35 years old), which mixes this heritage with exuberant joy and religious reverence."
Tiganá Santana (www.tigana.com.br, www.myspace.com/avozdetigana), a composer and singer from Salvador.

Pimentinha, Boca do Rio. One of the few clubs to be lively on a Mon.
Teatro Sesi Rio Vermelho, R Borges dos Reis 9, T071-3334 0668. One of the best venues in the city for contemporary Bahian bands.

⚙ Entertainment

Salvador *p20, maps p21, p25, p30 and p34*
The Fundação Cultural do Estado da Bahia edits *Bahia Cultural*, a monthly brochure listing the main cultural events for the month. These can be found in most hotels and Bahiatursa information centres. Local newspapers *A Tarde* and *Correio da Bahia* have good listing for cultural events in the city.

Cinema
The main shopping malls show mainstream Hollywood and international films, almost invariably dubbed (*dublado*). Only a few showings have subtitles (*legendas*).

Live music
Theatro Castro Alves, Largo 2 de Julho, Campo Grande, T071-3339 8000. The city's most distinguished performance space, home of the Bahian Symphony Orchestra and the Castro Alves Ballet Company. Also hosts performances by more cerebral MPB artists and contemporary performers like Hermeto Pascoal or Egberto Gismonti.

⚙ Festivals

Salvador *p20, maps p21, p25, p30 and p34*
6 Jan Epiphany. Public holiday with many free concerts and events. Beautiful Masses in many of the historic churches.
Jan Festa do Nosso Senhor do Bonfim. Held on the 2nd Sun after Epiphany. On the preceding Thu there is a colourful parade at the church with many penitents and a ceremonial washing of the church itself. Great for photographs.
Feb Carnaval, see box, page 48. The next carnival dates are 13-18 Feb 2015; 5-10 Feb 2016; and 24 Feb-1 Mar 2016.
2 Feb Pescadores do Rio Vermelho. Boat processions with gifts for Yemanjá, Goddess of the Sea, accompanied by African Brazilian music.
Mar/Apr Holy Week. The week before Easter sees many colourful processions around the old churches in the upper city.

Cachoeira *p38*
24 Jun São João, 'Carnival of the Interior.' Celebrations include dangerous games with fireworks, well attended by tourists.
Mid-Aug Nossa Sehora da Boa Morte.
4 Dec A famous *candomblé* ceremony at the Fonte de Santa Bárbara.

O Shopping

Salvador *p20, maps p21, p25, p30 and p34*

Arts, crafts and cigars

Artesanato Santa Bárbara, R Alfredo Brito 7, Pelourinho, T071-3321 2685. Excellent handmade lace.

Atelier Totonho and Raimundo, Ladeira do Carmo, Pelourinho. 2 adjacent galleries run by a co-operative of some 28 naïve art artists, including Totonho, Calixto, Raimundo Santos and Jô. Good prices.

FIEB-SESI, Av Tiradentes 299, Bonfim; Av Borges dos Reis 9, Rio Vermelho; and Av 7 de Setembro 261, Mercês. Some of the best artisan products in the city ranging from textiles and ceramics to musical instruments.

Goya Lopes, R Gregorio de Mattos, Pelourinho, T071-3321 9428, www. goyalopes.com.br. African-Brazilian designer clothing on Goya's Didara label, which features very simple, rustic cotton clothing and beach shawls stamped with intricate motifs in very bright colours from Afro-Brazilian cultural life.

Instituto Mauá, R Gregorio de Matos 27, Pelourinho. Tue-Sat 0900-1800, Sun 1000-1600. Good-quality items, better value and quality than the Mercado Modelo.

Loja de Artesanato do SESC, Largo Pelourinho, T071-3321 5502. Mon-Fri 0900-1800 (closed for lunch), Sat 0900-1300.

Oficina de Investigação Musical, Alfredo Brito 24, Pelourinho, T071-3322 2386. Mon-Fri 0800-1200 and 1300-1600. Handmade traditional percussion instruments (and percussion lessons for US$15 per hr).

Rosa do Prado, R Inacio Aciolly 5, Pelourinho. Cigar shop packed with every kind of Brazilian *charuto* imaginable.

Bookshops

Graúna, Av 7 de Setembro 1448, and R Barão de Itapoã 175, Porto da Barra. English titles.

Livraria Brandão, R Ruy Barbosa 4, Centre, T071-3243 5383. Second-hand English, French, Spanish and German books.

Jewellery

Casa Moreira, Ladeira da Praça, just south of Praça da Sé. Exquisite jewellery and antiques. Most are expensive, but there are some affordable charms.

Scala, Praça da Sé, T071-3321 8891. Handmade jewellery using locally mined gems (eg aquamarine, amethyst and emerald), workshop at back.

Markets

Feira de Artesanato, Santa Maria Fort. Wed 1700-2100. Arts and crafts in the fort at the far end of Porto da Barra beach.

Feira de São Joaquim, 5 km from Mercado Modelo along the seafront. Daily 0800-1900, Sun 0800-1200. The largest and least touristy market in the city selling mainly foodstuffs and a few artisan products. Very smelly.

Mercado Modelo, Praça Cairu, Cidade Baixa. Sat 0800-1900, Sun 0800-1200. Live music and dancing, especially Sat. Expect to be asked for money if you take photos. Many tourist items such as woodcarvings, silver-plated fruit, leather goods, local musical instruments. Lace items for sale are often not handmade (despite labels), are heavily marked up, and are much better bought at their place of origin (eg Ilha de Maré, Pontal da Barra and Marechal Deodoro).

Music and carnival souvenirs

Boutique Olodum, Praça José Alencar, Pelourinho. Olodum CDs, music, T-shirts and musical instruments.

Cana Brava records, R João de Deus 22, T071-3321 0536, www.bahia-online.net. Great little CD shop with a friendly and knowledgeable American owner. Stocks a whole range of classy Brazilian artists, less internationally famous names and back catalogue artists.

Ilê Aiyê, R das Laranjeiras 16, T071-3321
4193, www.ileaiye.org.br. Bags, clothes,
books, music and other such items from
this famous Carnaval drum orchestra
and *bloco*.

Shopping centres
These are the most comfortable places
to shop in Salvador – havens of a/c cool
in the heat of the Bahian summer offering
a chance to rest over an ice-cold beer,
to lunch and to shop for essentials like
Havaianas, bikinis, CDs and beach wraps
along with comestibles like batteries,
supermarket food and sunscreen.
Shopping Barra, Av Centenário 2992,
Chame-Chame, Barra, T071-2108 8288,
www.shoppingbarra.com. The largest
shopping mall within easy access of the
tourist centres.
Shopping Iguatemi, Av Tancredo Neves
148, Caminho das Árvores, T071-2126 1111,
www.iguatemisalvador.com.br. Next to the
rodoviária, with a broad spread of mid- to
upmarket shops, a large a/c food court and
cinemas on the top floor.
Salvador Shopping, Av Tancredo Neves
3133, Caminho das Árvores, www.salvador
shopping.com.br. One of the city's largest,
plushest and newest with an excellent
cinema and the best selection of upper-
end brands.

⏱ What to do

Salvador *p20, maps p21, p25, p30
and p34*
Capoeira
There are many capoeira schools offering
classes in and around the Pelourinho.
Associação de Capoeira Mestre Bimba,
R das Laranjeiras 1, Pelourinho, T071-3322
0639, www.capoeiramestrebimba.com.br.
This school is the inheritor of the teaching
of Mestre Bimba, who was the first master
to define a system for teaching capoeira
regional. There are both male and
female teachers.

**Escola de Capoeira Angola Irmãos
Gêmeos**, R Gregório de Mattos 9,
Pelourinho, T071-3321 0396/9963 3562,
http://ecaig.blogspot.com (also on
Facebook). A school founded by Mestre
Curió, who learnt with another legendary
capoeirista, Mestre Pastinha. Classes
are broad and are good for women,
children and older people. In Curió's
absence classes are conducted by the
mestre's pupil, Mestra Jararaca (the
first woman to earn the Mestra
title in Capoeira Angola).
Forte de Santo Antônio Alem do Carmo,
T071-3117 1488, www.fortesantantonio.
blogspot.com. Has a number of schools
teaching capoeira, usually in the evenings.
They include **Pele da Bahia**, T071-3387
6485, www.mestrepeledabahia.blogspot.
com, and **Mestre Boca Rica**, T071-
3401 3019.
**Grupo Cultural de Capoeira Angola
Moçambique**, R Gregório de Mattos 38,
Pelourinho, T071-8113 7455. Offers tuition
in Capoeira Angola. Teaching is very
flexible, with options for either day classes
or full terms and it also offers berimbau
and percussion lessons. Famous teachers
include mestres Boca Rica and Neco –
alumni of Canjiquinha and Waldemar –
2 of the most celebrated teachers of
the 20th century.

Football
**Fonte Nova – Otávio Mangabeira
Stadium**, Trav Joaquim Maurício, Nazaré,
T071-3242 3322. 90,000-seat stadium
which is home to the **Esporte Clube Bahia**
and **Vitória** football clubs. 10 mins away
from the Pelourinho, and the Barroquinha
terminal and fully rebuilt for 2014.

Music and percussion
Diaspora, R da Laranjeiras 44, T071-9998
8488. Afternoon and evening *afoxe*, samba
and *axê* dance, percussion music classes and
other courses on African Bahia (including
candomble). Classes from US$5 depending

on numbers (minimum 2 people) when bought in a block of several classes.
Escola do Olodum, R das Laranjeiras 30, T071-3322 8069. Classes from the masters of the Olodum school itself. Minimum 10 people, US$40 per hr per person.

Tour operators
Bus tours are available from several companies, including: **Alameda Turismo**, R Fernando Menezes de Góes 397, Pituba, T071-2107 5999, US$25 per person; and **Tours Bahia**, Largo do Cruzeiro de São Francisco 4/6, Centro Histórico, T071-3320 3280, www.toursbahia.com.br.
Cultour, R João Gomes, 88 Sala 8 Sobrado da Praça, Rio Vermelho, T071-3335 1062, www.cultour.it. Offers some of the best cultural tours in the city. Less 'touristy' than operators in the Pelourinho area.
Ilha Bela, Av da França, T071-3326 7158, www.ilhabelatm.com.br. Tours around the Baía de Todos os Santos and transfers to Morro de São Paulo.
Tatur Turismo, Av Tancredo Neves 274, Centro Empresarial Iguatemi, Salas 222-224, T071-3114 7900, www.tatur.com.br. Excellent private tours of the city and the state as well as general travel agency services including flight booking and accommodation. Can organize entire packages prior to arrival for the whole of Brazil. Good English, reliable. Irish-owned.

Ilha de Itaparica *p37*
Tour operators
Small boats for trips around the bay can be hired privately at the small port by the Mercado Modelo in Salvador. A pleasant trip out to the mouth of the bay should take 1½ hrs as you sail along the bottom of the cliff. When arranging to hire any boat check that the boat is licensed by the port authority (Capitânia dos Portos) and that there are lifejackets on board.
Companhia de Navegação Bahiana, T071-3321 7100. Sails 5 times a week to Maragojipe on the Rio Paraguaçu to the west (see page 55). The trip across the bay and up the valley of the river takes 3 hrs. There are some very beautiful views along the way with 2 stops. A good trip would be to continue to Cachoeira by bus from Maragojipe and return to Salvador the following day. Departures from Salvador from the Terminal Turístico in front of the Mercado Modelo, Mon-Thu 1430 (1530 in summer). Fri departure is at 1130. Departures from Maragojipe Mon-Thu 0500 and Fri 0830, US$4.50.
Steve Lafferty, R do Sodré 45, apt 301, T071-3241 0994. A US yachtsman, highly recommended for enjoyable sailing trips around Salvador, for up to 4 people.

Recôncavo Baiano *p38*
Recommended local tour guide **Claudio**, T075-3982 6080, doesn't speak much English, but is friendly and knowledgeable.

⊖ Transport

Salvador *p20, maps p21, p25, p30 and p34*
Air
To get to the airport: a/c *combis* leave from Praça da Sé bus stop via the coast road and Barra 0630-2100, US$4, 1-1½ hrs (1 hr from Barra). Ordinary buses marked 'Aeroporto' run from the same stop and cost US$1.50. A taxi to the airport costs around US$30 (US$35-40 after 2200 and on weekends and public holidays). Travel agencies and some hotels can also organize transfers.

There are domestic flights to all of Brazil's major cities, some with connections through **Recife**, **Belo Horizonte** or **São Paulo**; the best prices are usually to **Rio de Janeiro** and **São Paulo**. There are international flights to **Madrid** (3 times weekly with **Air Europa**), **Frankfurt** (once weekly with **Condor**), **Lisbon** (daily with **TAP**), **Milan** (once weekly with **Air Italy**) and weekly flights to **Miami** in the USA with **American Airlines**.

Airlines flying from Salvador include: **Addey**, www.addey.com.br; **Avianca**, www.avianca.com.br, **Azul**, http://viajemais.voeazul.com.br; **Gol**, www.voegol.com.br; and **TAM**, www.tam.com.br. International flights are with: **Air Europa**, www.aireuropa.com; **Condor**, www10.condor.com; and **TAP**, www.flytap.com.

Bus

Local Standard buses cost US$1.50 single; a/c *executivos* cost US$2-3 depending on the route. On buses and at the ticket sellers' booths, watch your change and beware of pickpockets (one scam used by thieves is to descend from the bus while you are climbing aboard). For details on buses in Salvador visit www.transalvador.salvador.ba.gov.br/transporte.

Buses marked 'Barra' and 'Campo Grande-Praça da Sé' run between the **Praça da Sé** in the Centro Histórico and **Barra**. There are a number of lines including M024-00 and M024-01 (both via R Carlos Gomes, Av 7 de Setembro and Praça 2 Julho in Campo Grande).

To get between the **airport** and Centro Histórico, Barra and the beaches, catch the S002-00 'Aeroporto-Praça da Sé' bus, which leaves from the **Praça da Se**, passing Av 7 de Setembro (Centre), Av 7 de Setembro and Av Oceânica in **Barra**, Av Oceânica in **Ondina**, R Paciencia, R João Gomes and R Osvaldo Cruz in **Rio Vermelho**, continuing on through **Amaralina**, **Pituba** and **Itapoã**, before turning in to the airport (1st bus 0500, last bus 2210). The 1002-00 'Aeroporto-Campo Grande' bus follows a similar route beginning at Av 7 de Setembro in the centre (1st bus 0545, last bus 2300). The most comfortable and quickest of these buses are the a/c *frescão*.

For the ocean beaches, take buses S011-00, S011-01 and S011-02 marked 'Praça da Sé-Flamengo'. These run to **Flamengo Beach** (30 km from the city), following the coastal route, passing through **Campo Grande** and **Barra** and all the best beaches

(including **Stella Maris** and **Itapoã**), and leaving from Praça da Sé, US$3.50; sit on the right-hand side for the best views (1st 0600, last 1930). For **Bonfim** and **Ribeira**, take one of the following: bus S021-00 marked 'Ribeira-Pituba' calls at Ribeira, R Imperatriz, next to the Igreja do Bonfim, Av da Franca 200 m north of the Mercado Modelo, Av Juracy Magalhaes Jr in Rio Vermelho and Pituba Beach; 'Bus S027-00' marked 'Ribeira Campo Grande' calls at Ribeira, the Ladeira do Bonfim near the church, R Itapicuru at R Jacuipe in Mont Serrat, Av da Franca 200 m north of the Mercado Modelo, R Carlos Gomes and the Av 7 Setembro in the centre and in Campo Grande (near the Mosteiro São Bento) and Av Setembro in Barra. Bus 0219-00 runs between Ribeira and the *rodoviária*, leaving from R Travas Fora in Bonfim.

Long distance To get to the *rodoviária* take bus RI or RII, 'Centro-Rodoviária-Circular' (US$1), from the Lower City at the foot of the Lacerda Lift; the journey can take up to 1 hr, especially at peak periods. On weekdays, a quicker executive bus (US$2) runs from Praça da Sé or Praça da Inglaterra (by McDonalds), Comércio, to **Iguatemi Shopping Centre** from where there is a walkway to the *rodoviária* (take care in the dark). Alternatively take a bus from the centre, US$15.

There are frequent services to the majority of destinations; a large panel in the main hall of the bus terminal lists destinations and the relevant ticket office. For bus information contact the *rodoviária*, Av Antônio Carlos Magalhães 4362, T071-3460 8300, daily 0600-2200, and see www.itapemerim.com.br, www.aguiabranca.com.br, www.real expresso.com.br and www.gontijo.com.br.

To **Aracaju**, 3 daily (1st 0630, last 2200), 4½ hrs, US$29, *leito* US$35 with Bomfim. To **Belém**, US$55 *comercial* with Itapemirim. To **Ilhéus**, 8 daily, 7 hrs, US$36, *executivo* US$46, *leito* US$80 with Bomfim. To **Maceio**, 4 daily, 1st at 0630, last 2200,

4½ hrs, US$42, *leito* US$67 with **Bomfim**. To **Porto Seguro**, 1 daily at 2000, 10 hrs, US$77 with **Aguia Branca**. To **Recife**, US$90, 13 hrs, 1 daily and 1 *leito*, with Itapemerim, T071-3358 0037. To **Rio de Janeiro**, Mon-Sat 0700, 26 hrs, US$125, *leito* US$145, with **Itapemirim** and **Aguia Branca**; good stops, clean toilets, recommended. To **São Paulo**, 30 hrs, US$120, US$155, with São Geraldo (Mon, Wed and Fri at 0830 and 1930, Sun, Mon and Sat at 2000), daily *leito* at 2200. To **Fortaleza**, 20 hrs, US$105 at 0900 with **Itapemerim**. To **Lençóis** at 2200, 6-8 hrs, US$30 with **Real Expresso**, via Feira de Santana, T071-3358 1591. To **Belo Horizonte**, Gontijo, T071-3358 7448, at 1700, US$120. There are also bus services to **Brasília** along the fully paved BR-242, via **Barreiras**, 3 daily, 23 hrs; **Palmas**, **Natal**, **João Pessoa**, **Penedo** (via **Maceio**), **Vitória** and **Teresina**. For the shortest route to **Valença**, take the ferry from São Joaquim to Bom Despacho on Itaparica island, from where it is 130 km to Valença via **Nazaré das Farinhas** (see page 38).

Car hire
There are various car hire booths in the airport: **Hertz**, www.hertz.com.br, **Interlocadora**, www.interlocadora.com.br, and **Localiza**, www.localiza.com.

Taxi
Meters start at US$1.50 and then US$0.70 per 100 m. They charge US$25 per hr within city limits, and 'agreed' rates outside. Taxi Barra-Centro, US$10 daytime; US$12 at night. Watch the meter; the night-time charge should be 30% higher than daytime charges. **Teletaxi** (24-hr service), T071-3321 9988.

Ferry and boat
See also Getting there, page 22, and Ilha de Itaparica, page 37. Boats and catamarans to **Ilha de Itaparica** and other islands in the Baía de Todos os leave from the main ferry dock, **Marítimo de São Joaquim**, Av

Oscar Pontes 1051, T071-3254 1020, www.twbmar.com.br. There are 10 car ferries per day to Itaparica. Passenger boats for Itaparica and **Morro de São Paulo** (2½ hrs) leave from Salvador's other boat terminal, the **Terminal Marítimo de Mercado Modelo** (or Terminal Marítimo Turístico). See www.morrodesaopaulo.com.br for the latest ferry timetables.

Ilha de Itaparica *p37*
Ferry
There are regular ferry services to **Salvador**. The main passenger ferry leaves from Bom Despacho and runs to the **Marítimo de São Joaquim** ferry dock. The 1st ferry to Salvador is at 0515 and the last one at 2300, running at intervals of 45 mins, During the summer months the ferries are much more frequent. (Buses for **Calçada**, Ribeira, stop across the road from the ferry terminal; the 'Sabino Silva–Ribeira' bus passes in front of the Shopping Barra). Enquiries at **Companhia de Navegação Bahiana (CNB)**, T071-3321 7100, open 0800-1700. A one-way ticket for foot passengers Mon-Fri is US$1, Sat and Sun US$1.20. There is also a catamaran service which departs from Bom Despacho twice daily, US$3.

From Mar Grande a smaller ferry (*lancha*) runs to the **Terminal Marítimo**, in front of the Mercado Modelo in Salvador. The ferries leave every 45 mins and the crossing takes 50 mins, US$3 return.

Recôncavo Baiano *p38*
Bus To **Salvador** (Camurjipe) every hr from 0530. To **Feira Santana**, 2 hrs, US$3.

● Directory

Salvador *p20, maps p21, p25, p30 and p34*
Banks Selected branches of major banks have ATMs (which accept Visa and Cirrus cards) and exchange facilities. All shopping centres, the bus station and the airport have branches of **Bradesco**, and

there is a branch at R Chile 23, T071-3321 3154. Changing money at banks (open 1000-1600) can be bureaucratic and time-consuming. **Citibank**, R Miguel Calmon 555, Comércio, centre, changes TCs. Branch at R Almte Marquês de Leão 71, Barra, has an ATM. **Banco do Brasil**, Av Estados Unidos 561, Comércio, in the shopping centre opposite the *rodoviária* (also a *câmbio* here), very high commission on TCs, at the airport on the 1st floor (Mon-Fri 0830-1530, 1600-2100 and Sat, Sun and holidays 0900-1600); branches in Barra, R Miguel Bournier 4, in Shopping Barra and in Ondina. **Cultural centres** Associação Cultural Brasil-Estados Unidos, Av 7 de Setembro 1883, has a library and reading room with recent US magazines, open to all, free use of internet for 30 mins. **Cultura Inglesa**, R Plínio Moscoso 357, Jardim Apipema. **German Goethe Institut**, Av 7 de Setembro 1809, also with a library and reading room. **Immigration** Polícia Federal, Av O Pontes 339, Aterro de Água de Meninos, Lower City, T071-3319 6082. Open 1000-1600. For extensions of entry permits show an outward ticket or sufficient funds for your stay, visa extension

US$15. **Internet** There are numerous internet cafés throughout the touristy parts of the city. **Language courses** Casa do Brasil, R Milton de Oliveira 231, Barra, T071-3264 5866, www.casadobrazil.com. br. Portuguese for foreigners. **Diálogo**, R Dr João Pondé 240, Barra, T071-3264 0007, www.dialogo-brazilstudy.com, with optional dance, *capoeira* and cooking classes and accommodation arranged with host families. **Superlearning Idiomas**, Av 7 de Setembro 3402, Ladeira da Barra, T071-3337 2824, www.allways.com.br/spl. **Laundry** Kit Lavaderia, Av Amaralina 829, Amaralina. **Laundromat**, R Oswaldo Cruz, Rio Vermelho. **Lav e Lev**, Av Manoel Dantas da Silva 2364, loja 7. **Unilave**, Av Magalhães Neto 18, Pituba. **Medical services** Clinic, Barão de Loreto 21, Graça. **Delegação Federal de Saúde**, R Padre Feijó, Canela. Free yellow fever vaccinations.

Cachoeira *p38*
Banks Bradesco, in the main square, ATM accepts Visa credit but not debit cards, Mon-Fri 0830-1700. **Post office** In the main square, Mon-Fri 0900-1700.

Cocoa and Dendê coasts

South of Salvador and the Recôncavo, Bahia descends in a series of glorious beaches, offshore islands and jungly peninsulas, many of them fringed with coral and mangrove or backed by endless kilometres of coconut palms. Sluggish tropical rivers undulate their way across lowland Bahia from the Chapada Diamantina ('diamond mountains') of the interior and interrupt the coastline, while potholed roads connect crumbling colonial towns like Ilhéus and Olivença, which grew fat on the cocoa and dendê oil trade but have since been slowly withering under the tropical sun.

The glorious coast is within easy reach of Salvador and every year an increasing number of tourists are discovering its forgotten fishing villages. The surf mecca of Itacaré is gradually turning chic. The expat community of Morro de São Paulo, on the island of Tinharé, is finding its beach haven is getting crowded; the nightlife here is notoriously lively. Those seeking seclusion should head for the Peninsula de Maraú, a little further south, or to the little-explored wild beaches beyond Una.

Tinharé and Morro de São Paulo → For listings, see pages 63-70.

Depending on whom you ask, Tinharé is either a single large island separated from the mainland by the estuary of the Rio Una and mangrove swamps, or a mini archipelago divided by estuaries, mangroves and an impossibly turquoise sea. Either way it is stunning: a semi-wilderness of bird-filled Mata Atlântica forest fringed with swaying coconut palms and white-sand beaches that until recently were known only to fishermen and a few intrepid Brazilian beach travellers. Before the 1990s the main town here, Morro de São Paulo, on the northern tip of the island, was one of the world's great secret tropical island getaways. Now it is rapidly becoming as over-developed as a Thai beach and many of the original fishermen who lived on the gorgeous beaches that line Tinharé have already been relocated. Every beach for 20 km south of Morro town is now backed by hotels and Morro has become a veritable tourist hotspot.

Morro Town itself is dominated by a lighthouse and the ruins of an early 17th-century colonial fort, built as a defence against European raiders. However, this did not stop the Dutch and French using the waters around the island as hiding places for attacks on the Portuguese and even establishing bases here for brief periods of time.

Morro de São Paulo

Morro sits right at the northern tip of Tinharé. Boats from Salvador arrive at a jetty and travellers enter the town through the stone arch that once marked the gateway to the fortress. The battlements are now largely in ruin, perched on top of the craggy hill in front of a series of little streets that branch off a small colonial *praça*. The main thoroughfare runs south to the town's beaches. Another path runs north to the lighthouse and a ruined lookout post complete with cannon (dolphins can be seen in August) and along the beaches to the village of **Gamboa**, which retains a strong local character and which has another magnificent. From Gamboa it's possible to visit the **Fonte de Ceu** waterfall; make sure you check the tide times, or ask around for a guide. It's possible to walk or take one of the regular boats that run between Gamboa and Morro every 30-60 minutes (depending on the time of day), US$1.50.

Morro has five beaches; are all idyllic but are quieter the further from town you go. There is swimming in the sea or in the saltwater coral pools that appear at low tide. The beaches are named prosaically: **Primeira** (first), **Segunda** (second), **Terceira** (third), **Quarta** (fourth) and **Quinta** (fifth). There are boardwalks and a heavy build-up of shacks, beach bars, restaurants and hotels all the way to Terceira. Primeira is barely a beach at all and has the bulk of the hotels. Segunda is a party beach and is very popular with 20-somethings. Quinta is the furthest from town and is the quietest with little noise but the gentle lap of the sea. Before deciding to walk all the way to Quinta (1½ to two hours) check the tide times as the beach gets cut off at high tide. On 7 September there is a big festival at Morro with live music on the beach.

Arriving in Tinharé and Morro de São Paulo

Getting there There are direct 20-minute flights from Salvador's airport to the third beach at Morro de São Paulo with **Addey Taxi Aereo** ① *T075-3652 1242, www.addey.comtur.br*, which flies three times daily and costs around US$110 return. Catamarans run from both of Salvador's ferry terminals (see pages 55 and 69), taking around two hours, US$40; times vary according to the weather but there are usually several a day 0800-1400; check with the tourist office or **Catamarã Gamboa do Morro** ① *T075-9975 6395*. Part of the trip is on the open sea, which can be rough. There are also numerous water taxis. Modified fishing and speed boats also run from Salvador via **Valença** (an unprepossessing town on the mainland served by regular buses from Salvador and southern Bahia) and Itaparica. The website www. morrodesaopaulo.com.br has useful information in English, Spanish and Italian including the latest boat times. There is a port tax of US$0.50 payable at the *dock* on leaving Morro or Gamboa (though in practice the staff are rarely there). ›› *See Transport, page 69.*

Getting around Morro is tiny and the first four beaches are easily negotiable on foot. A walk from town to Quarta Praia takes around 40 minutes. Until 2008 all roads were sand or dirt tracks but there is now a partially paved section between the town and the beaches, and this is plied by regular VW buses, motorbikes and beach buggies. These leave from the **Receptivo**, a little café that marks the beginning of the road just behind the second and third beaches; it's not hard to find but if in doubt ask for '*Receptivo*' or '*a estrada*'. There are daily transfers to Boipeba by Toyota at 0930, bookable through hotels or the myriad agencies on the island.

Boat trips around Tinharé island can be organized through hotels or agencies in the village; a full day costs US$20-30. Most of these go in a clockwise direction around Tinharé, visiting Boipeba and the villages to the south (including Moreré), the offshore reef pools for snorkelling, followed by the tiny colonial town of Cairu on the mainland and the shores of the Mangrove-line Rio Cairu, before returning.

Best time to visit Morro is expensive between December and March and gets very crowded during public holidays and prices can more than double. Beware of drug dealers and robbery at the busiest times.

Tourist Information There is a tourist booth, **Centro de Informações ao Turista** (CIT) ① *Praça Aureliano Lima s/n, T075-3652 1083, www.morrosp.com.br.* However, the website www.morrodesaopaulo.com.br is more useful and provides lists of agencies, hotels and other information in several languages.

Ilha de Boipeba → *For listings, see pages 63-70.*

Ilha de Boipeba, a few hours south of Morro, is a similar but far quieter island and with less infrastructure. Accommodation is grouped in three places: the little town on the banks of the Rio do Inferno where the ferry arrives; the adjacent beach, **Boca da Barra**, which is more idyllic; and the fishing village of **Moreré**, a 30-minute boat ride to the south (only possible at high tide). With just a few simple restaurants and a football field on the beach overlooking a beautiful turquoise bay, life here is tranquil even by Bahian standards. Expect to pay at least US$30 for a boat to Moreré. Walking along the beaches will take about two hours. Have your camera at the ready, bring sunscreen and go at low tide as there is a river to ford.

Arriving on Ilha de Boipeba Boat trips leave daily from Morro de São Paulo at 0900; book through a travel agent or your hotel. The return journey costs around US$30, and you have to pay this even if you are intending to stay on the island. Tractors and 4WDs leave from Morro's second beach every morning at around 0800 (one hour, US$15), and return at midday; contact **Zé Balacha** ① *T075-9148 0343*, or ask at your hotel.

South to Itacaré → *For listings, see pages 63-70.*

Ituberá and Camamu → *Phone code: 073.*

These two towns, which have yet to be overrun by seasonal visitors, are the first stops south on the bus route from Valença. Neither have good beaches but both have access to decent ones by boat. **Ituberá** is a tiny town sitting on a deep inlet; the most beautiful beach in the area, **Barra do Carvalho**, is two hours away by boat. Some 30 km further south, **Camamu** is tucked away in a maze of mangroves. It is the jumping-off point for the peninsula of **Maraú** – the next stretch of the Bahian coast in line for beach resort development. The town has a handful of pretty colonial buildings, including the 17th-century church of Nossa Senhora da Assunção.

Barra Grande and the Peninsula de Maraú → *Phone code: 073.*

This long thin peninsula stretches north from the town of Maraú, near Itacaré, towards the southern extremity of the island of Tinharé and is fringed with beautiful beaches along its entire length both on the ocean side and along the beautiful Baía de Camamu. The bay is lined with thick mangrove at its far southern end and sealed at **Tremembé**, with a plunging waterfall that cascades directly into the sea. The main centre of population is

Itacaré beaches north to south

Do Pontal Immediately across the Rio de Contas from town and reached by passenger ferry. Long, deserted and stretching all the way to Barra Grande some 40 km away – if you're prepared to swim across rivers and camp out.

Coroinha At the harbour, urban and none too clean but with pretty views of the town and the 18th-century church of São Miguel, especially at sunset.

Da Concha Urban and with the bulk of the *pousadas*.

Do Resende A little bay with powdery white sand, swaying coconut palms and a handful of *pousadas*. 10 minutes' walk from Da Concha.

Tiririca The best surf beach in Itacaré, *pousadas* with a beatnik surfer crowd. 10 minutes' walk from Resende.

Do Costa A little bay with strong waves and reasonable surf. 10 minutes' walk from Tiririca.

Do Ribeira The end of the road from town. Very pretty with calm water and rainforest rising at each end. Beach *barracas* sell fish and snacks and there's a little stream for kids. 10 minutes' walk from Do Costa.

Prainha More private and accessible by trail from Ribeira. Good surf. In a protected area (US$1.50 entry fee). 20-30 minutes' walk from Do Ribeira.

the little fishing village of **Barra Grande** at the tip of the peninsula, fronted by a glorious beach and yachts bobbing at the end of a pier. The sandy streets are lined with a handful of *pousadas* and shaded by *casuaring* and palms. Few non-Brazilian tourists make it here.

Arriving in Barra Grande and the Peninsula de Maraú The peninsula is 200 km south of Salvador, 150 km north of Ilhéus. There is a small airport at Barra Grande, served by scheduled air taxis from Morro de São Paulo and Salvador. Boats run from Camamu to Barra Grande several times a day between October and March and once a day in the morning all year round (boats: one hour, US$3; *lancha*: 20 minutes, US$15). It's also possible to reach the peninsula by road from Itacaré.

Access is difficult to many of the Maraú beaches if you don't have a car (and only possible with a 4WD in wet weather), but some can be reached on foot or by taxi/*combi* from Barra Grande. Tractors run from the village to the more remote beaches further south. There are excellent two- to five-day tours with **Orbitá** (see page 69), leaving from Ilhéus or Itacaré. There are plenty of *pousadas* in Barra (see Where to stay, page 65); the website www.barragrande.net has lots of useful information.

Itacaré → *Phone code: 073.*
Itacaré is a pretty little surfer town at the far end of the Peninsula de Maraú surrounded by glorious forest-fringed beaches. Paulistanos decided it was cool at the turn of the millennium and a handful of beaches are now backed by some of Bahia's most exclusive (and increasingly oversized) resorts, such as **Txai**. Those close to the town itself are more hippy, with an informal surfer-dude feel and a mix of cheaper restaurants and places to stay and more fashionable spots for those swooping in for the evening. Much of the old town remains a simple fishing village whose houses in thick *gouache* shades huddle together under a golden sun around a broad harbour on the banks of the Rio de Contas.

Arriving in Itacaré The *rodoviária* is a few minutes walk from town. There are at least four buses a day from Ilhéus (one hour). Porters are on hand with wheelbarrows to help with luggage. For information contact the **Secretaria de Turismo de Itacaré** ① *T073-3251 2134, www.itacare.com.br*. *Pousadas* are concentrated on and around **Praia da Concha**, the first beach south of the town centre and the river. More deserted beaches lie along dirt roads to the south and north. To explore the area to the full you will need a car. If you speak some Portuguese, it's worth taking the time to find your way to one of the smaller places. Itacaré is very busy with Brazilian tourists in high season but receives relatively few international visitors.

Ilhéus and around → *For listings, see pages 63-70. Phone code: 073. Population: 242,500.*

Everyone is happy to point out that Ilhéus is the birthplace of Jorge Amado (1912) and the setting of one of his most famous novels: *Gabriela, Cravo e Canela* (Gabriela, Clove and Cinnamon, 1958). Amado also chronicled life on the region's cocoa plantations in two novels, *Cacau* (1933), and the much better-known *Terras do Sem Fim* (The Violent Lands, 1942). A later novel, *São Jorge dos Ilhéus* (1944), continues the story.

Ilhéus's history stretches back to the earliest days of Portuguese colonization, when it was one of the captaincies created by King João III in 1534. Today the port serves a district that produces 65% of all Brazilian cocoa. Shipping lines call regularly. There are good views of the city from the **Convento de Nossa Senhora da Piedade**. Most tourists stay for an hour or two before heading north towards Itacaré or south towards Porto Seguro.

The town has a number of sights. The church of **São Jorge** ① *Praça Rui Barbosa*, (1556), is the city's oldest and has a small museum. The cathedral of **São Sebastião** ① *Praça Dom Eduardo*, is a huge, early 20th-century building. In Alto da Vitória is the 17th-century **Nossa**

Ilhéus

To Rodoviária & Itabuna
To 4 & Malhado
Teresópolis
Lad Teresópolis
Conquista
da Rocha
7 de Setembro
Lad Vitória
Praça Castro Alves
Bento Berito
M. Vitória
Av Soares Lopes
Praça Barbosa
Praça Coronel Pessoa
Praça Rui Barbosa
São Jorge
AC Lemos
Dantas
Câmara
Praia da Avenida
Tiradentes
Dendé
Eloy
Praça Seabra
Prefeitura
Jorge Amado
Casa Jorge Amado
Terminal Urbana
Praça Cairu
Marquês de Paranaguá
Pedro II
Sá
Paiva
Prof Amélia Nunes
& Orbita Tours
E Bastos
Av Almirante Linhares
Cathedral
Av Z
ar ap Ilho
Praça Dom Eduardo
Bataclã
Atlantic Ocean
Baía do Pontal
To Pontal, Airport, Olivença & Armação
To 5

N
Not to scale

Where to stay 🛏
Barravento 4
Britânia 1
Jardim Atlântico 5

Restaurants 🍴
Acarajé de Irene 1
Vesúvio 4

Senhora da Vitória, built to celebrate a victory over the Dutch. The house where Jorge Amado grew up and wrote his first novel is now a small **museum** ① *R Jorge Amado 21, 0900-1600, US$1*. Immortalized by Amado in *Gabriela, Cravo e Canela*, the **Bataclã** ① *Av 2 de Julho 75, T073-3634 7835*, was once a famous bordello and poker palace. It was used by the region's powerful cacão *coroneis* and linked to other parts of the town by a series of secret tunnels, through which (presumably) the macho men would flee in fear of their wives.

Arriving in Ilhéus The **airport** ① *3 km from the centre, in Pontal on the south bank of the river, linked to Ilhéus by bridge; taxi into town US$4*, receives flights from Salvador, Belo Horizonte, São Paulo, Brasília, Curitiba, Porto Seguro and Rio de Janeiro. The **rodoviária** ① *R Itabuna, 4 km from the centre*, has regular bus connections with Salvador. However, the Itabuna–Olivença bus runs through the centre of Ilhéus. The **tourist office** ① *on the beach opposite Praça Castro Alves*, is a few minutes' walk from the cathedral. Staff are friendly and can provide maps (US$2, recommended).

Around Ilhéus

The city beach itself is polluted but the beaches around the town are splendid and increasingly deserted the further you go. North of Ilhéus, two good beaches are **Marciano**, with reefs offshore and good surfing, and **Barra**, 1 km further north at the mouth of the Rio Almada. South of the river, the beaches at **Pontal** can be reached by 'Barreira' bus; alight just after the **Hotel Jardim Atlântico**. Between Ilhéus and **Olivença** are a number of fine beaches, including **Cururupe**, **Batuba** and **Cai n'Água** (in Olivença itself), both popular surf spots. The **Balneário de Tororomba** ① *on the Rio Batuba, 19 km from Ilhéus, bus from São Jorge, Canavieiras or Olivença*, has ferruginous mineral baths.

From Ilhéus, buses run every 30 minutes to **Itabuna** (32 km), the trading centre of the rich cocoa zone; there are also many lumber mills. **Ceplac installations** ① *Km 8, on the Itabuna–Ilhéus road, T073-214 3000, Mon-Fri 0830-1230*, demonstrates the processing of cocoa. Tours of cocoa plantations can be arranged through the **Ilhéus Praia** hotel.

Also at Km 8, the Projeto Mico-Leão Baiano at the **Reserva Biológica de Una** ① *www. ecoparque.org.br, book through Orbitá, see page 69*, was founded to protect the golden-faced tamarin. This is the wettest part of Bahia, most notably in October. Jeeps leave from the *rodoviária*. The reserve lies along a dirt road and most easily reached on a tour or by public jeep which leave when full from the *rodoviária*.

Beyond Ilhéus, the paved coastal road continues south through **Olivença** and **Una**, ending at **Canavieiras**, a picturesque town which benefited from the cocoa boom. It has several fine beaches worth exploring. A rough road continues from there to Porto Seguro.

Cocoa and Dendê coasts listings

For hotel and restaurant price codes and other relevant information, see pages 8-11.

⊖ Where to stay

Tinharé and Morro de São Paulo
p57

In **Morro de São Paulo**, there are many cheap *pousadas* and rooms to rent near the Fonte Grande (fountain), but this part of town does not get a breeze at night.

There are 4 beaches next to Morro town, which are quieter the further from town you go. The 1st and 2nd beaches are designated party areas, with throbbing bars and shacks selling food and drinks well into the night. There are only *pousadas* and a few restaurants on the final 2 beaches. To reach the beaches turn right at the end of the main street; there is only one trail out of town. You'll have to walk as there are no cars on the island; porters can be hired to transport your luggage to the hotel in a wheelbarrow.

$$$$ Hotel Vila dos Orixás, Praia do Encanto, T075-3652 2055, www.hotelvila dosorixas.com. A Spanish-run *pousada* on one of Morro's loneliest beaches with a series of spacious chalets set in a coconut garden, next to a pool and overlooking the beach. Very peaceful and romantic but a 30-min car ride from town. The hotel runs regular shuttles.

$$$$ Pousada Catavento, 4th beach, T075-3652 1052, www.cataventopraiahotel. com.br. One of the most luxurious and secluded of the hotels on the island, with well-appointed mock-colonial rooms arranged around a beautiful sculpted swimming pool, a decent restaurant and good service.

$$$$ Pousada da Torre, 2nd beach, T075-3652 1038, www.pousadadatorre.com.br. A very tasteful little boutique hotel on the beachfront which looks particularly enticing at night when both the building and the turquoise pool are mood lit under the palms. The plushest rooms are on the upper floor, are decked out in jaqueira wood and raw stone and have balconies with sea views behind big French windows. Rooms in the back annexe are a good deal cheaper, plainer but are large with king-sized beds and rich wood walls.

$$$ Agua Viva, 3rd beach, T075-3652 1217, www.pousadaaguavivamorro.com. br. The best rooms in this simple *pousada* are at the front and have little balconies overlooking the beach. They have a/c, fridges and TVs, polished concrete floors and are decorated with art painted by the Morro owners.

$$$ Fazenda Vila Guaiamú, 3rd beach, T075-3652 1035, www.vilaguaiamu.com. br. 7 tastefully decorated chalets of various sizes and styles set in their own tropical gardens and visited by marmosets, tanagers and rare cotingas. The hotel has a spa service with wonderful massage. The Italian photographer owner runs an ecotourism project protecting a rare species of crab, which live in the river that runs through the *fazenda*. Guided rainforest walks available. Excellent food. The best option for nature lovers.

$$$ Pousada Vistabella, 1st beach, T075-3652 1001, www.vistabelapousada.com. Good rooms, all with fans and hammocks. Rooms at the front have lovely views and are cooler. The owner Petruska is very welcoming. Recommended.

$$ Aradhia, 3rd beach, T075-8112 9150, facebook: pousada.aradhia. Spotlessly clean whitewash and white tile a/c rooms next to the beach, with space for a family of 4, small pool, Wi-Fi and Brazilian TV.

$$ Barra Vento, 3rd beach, T075-3652 1134, www.pousadabarraventa.com.br. Friendly and locally run *pousada* with slate floored a/c rooms, decked out with little more than a bed and fridge, but each has a small balcony, Wi-Fi and flatscreen cable TV.

Be sure to try the owner's barbecued pizza and see his collection of different sands from around the world.

$$ Coqueiro Do Caitá, 3rd beach, T075-3652 1194, www.coqueirodocaita.com. This little 2-storey hotel sits at the end of a leafy alleyway behind the beach and has a series of a/c rooms with little more than a bed and a fan, suites with a jacuzzi and a small swimming pool.

$$ Farol das Estrelas, 3rd beach, T075-8836 7088, www.faroldasestrelas.com. This squat, mock-colonial building huddled in a busy terrace of *pousadas* and restaurants has modest a/c rooms, some of which have balconies overlooking the beach and all of which are painted in soft, warm colours and decorated with local paintings. Staff are helpful and speak English, French and Italian. Great breakfast.

$$ Hostel Morro de São Paulo, R Fonte Grande at the end of Beco dos Pássaros, T075-3652 1521, www.hosteldomorro.com. br. This bright HI hostel with terraces slung with hammocks offers small dorms and doubles (which are more expensive than those in nearby guesthouses), a tiny pool and a booking service for tours around Morro.

$$ Pousada Colibri, R do Porto de Cima s/n, Centro, near the fountain, Morro de São Paulo. One of the few that stays cool in this part of town. 6 apartments with pleasant sea views. The owner, speaks English and German.

$$ Pousada Farol do Morro, 1st beach, T075-3652 1036, www.faroldomorro.com. br. Little huts running up a steep slope. All are a little small but have a sea view and are reached by a private funicular railway. The pool sits perched on the edge of the hill. Brazilian owned.

$$ Pousada Grauça, 3rd beach, T075-3652 1099, www.pousadagrauca.com.br. Simple but well-kept a/c and fan-cooled rooms with en suites in concrete *cabañas* away from the beach. Formerly called the 'Aradhia'. Recommended.

$$ Pousada Ilha da Saudade, 1st beach, T075-3652 1015, www.ilhadasaudade.com. br. Elegant hillside *pousada* with a beautiful pool with a view, a small gym and deluxe suites with jacuzzis. Restaurant, bar and good breakfast.

$$ Pousada Ilha do Sol, 1st beach, T075-8871 1295, www.pousadailhadosol.com. A big, blocky hotel with modest but well-kept rooms on long balcony corridors. The best have sea views. Generous breakfast.

$$ Tia Lita, 3rd beach, T075-3652 1532, www.pousadatialita.com.br. Very simple a/c rooms with television. Attentive, friendly service. Check a few rooms as some beds are spongy. Very good restaurant with delicious *moqueca de camarão*. Locally owned.

$ Pousada Timbalada, 2nd beach, T075-3652 1366, www.pousadatimbalada.com. br. A simple but welcoming guesthouse tucked away down an alley near party central on the 2nd beach. Small, brightly painted boxy rooms with hammock terraces and barely space for a backpack, and attractive raw stone and terracotta paint public areas.

Gamboa *p58*

$$$ Village do Dendê, Gamboa Beach, T075-3653 7104, www.villagedodende chales.yolasite.com. Well-appointed small chalets (each with a kitchenette and space for a family in 2 separate rooms), set in a lovely garden filled with dendê palms and heliconia flowers. Right next to the beach.

Ilha de Boipeba *p59*

Accommodation is split between the little town where the riverboat ferry arrives, the adjacent beach, **Boca da Barra**, which is more idyllic, and the fishing village of **Moreré**, 30-mins' boat ride to the south (high tide only).

$$$ Pousada Tassimirim, Tassimirim Beach (a 20- to 30-min walk south of town), T075-3653 6030, www.ilhaboipeba.org.br/ en/tassimirim.html. A coconut grove off the beach shades terracotta-roofed bungalows, an al fresco bar, restaurant and pool and a garden visited by dozens of hummingbirds. The price includes breakfast and dinner. Secluded and very tranquil.

$$$ Santa Clara, Boca da Barra Beach, T075-3653 6085, www.santaclaraboipeba. com. Californian-owned *pousada* with the island's best restaurant and large, tastefully decorated duplex *cabañas*. Very good-value room for 4 (**$** per person). Superlative therapeutic massages available.

$$$ Vila Sereia, Boca da Barra Beach, T075-3635 6045, www.ilhaboipeba.org.br/en/vilasereia.html. Elegantly simple wooden chalets overlooking the beach. Breakfast on your own private veranda. Very romantic.

$$ Horizonte Azul, Boca da Barra Beach, T075-3653 6080, www.pousadahorizonte azul.com. Pretty little *pousada* nextdoor to Santa Clara, with a range of chalets from very comfortable to fairly simple. The hillside garden is visited by hundreds of rare birds from the nearby Atlantic coast rainforest. Very friendly owners who speak English and French. Lunch available.

$ Geographic Hostel, Praça Santo Antônio 12, T075-3653 6104, ww.geographicboipeba.com.br. This turquoise blue concrete bungalow, set in gardens in Boipeba village has been converted into a small hostel with boxy dorms and doubles, a large sitting area and a terrace. There is Wi-Fi in public areas.

$ Sete, Praça Santo Antônio, Boipeba village, T075-3653 6135, www.ilhaboipeba. org.br/sete.html. This family-run 3-room *pousada* in the village is one of the cheapest options in Boipeba and offers small but very well-maintained a/c rooms with tiled floors and whitewashed walls decorated with floral prints.

Ituberá and Camamu *p59*

$$ Rio Acaraí, Praça Dr Francisco Xavier, T073-3255 2315, www.hotelrioacarai.com. br. Ugly modern *pousada* with a pool and restaurant.

$ Green House, next to the *rodoviária*, T073-3255 2178. Very basic and friendly with breakfast and a simple restaurant.

$ Tropical, Av Hildebrando Araújo Góes 270, Ituberá, T073-3256 2233. Standard, simple, small town *pousada* with a/c rooms, a restaurant, bar and pool.

Barra Grande and the Peninsula de Maraú *p59*

$$$$ Kiaroa, Praia Taipus de Fora, T073-3258 6213, www.kiaroa.com.br. The best of the peninsula's resorts, on a glorious beach, with a range of well-appointed rooms and an excellent restaurant, pampering and various organized activities.

$$$$ Lagoa do Cassange, Praia do Cassange (Caixa Postal 23), Camamu, T073-3255 2348, www.lagoadocassange.com.br. Cabins in a lawned garden between a wild stretch of beach and a lake populated with dozens of water bird species. A/c rooms have coffee-coloured walls, raw dark wood and wicker furniture. Bright raw cotton bedspreads, scatter cushions and rugs add splashes of colour. All have small verandas hung with hammocks. The hotel practises sustainable tourism by supporting local communities and undertaking some recycling.

$$$ Taipú de Fora, Praia Taipus de Fora, T073-3258 6278, www.taipudefora.com. br. Small upscale mini-resort with a good range of activities including diving and kayaking. The beach is glorious, little-known but one of Bahia's very best (and buried here in text so that only discerning readers will discover it!).

$$ Eco Village Picaranga, Rio Picaranga, Peninsula de Maraú, T073-9973 9692, www.piracanga.com. A holistic beachside retreat on the south of the peninsula 6 km north of Itacaré, offering treatments, workshops, courses, excursions and alternative weddings. Profits are shared with the local community. Accommodation is in comfortable thatched-roof chalets and bungalows and there is a large maloca-like community space for meditation and movement, a sauna and a wholefood restaurant.

$$ El Capitan, Av Vasco Neto s/n, a block from the beach at the mainland end of the town, 200 m from the pier, T073-3258 6078, www.elcapitan.com.br. Cabins in a garden decorated with rusting anchors and nautical bric-a-brac. All are basic in tile and concrete, have terracotta-tile roofs and hammock-slung terraces gathered around a pool.

$ Meu Sossego, R Dr Chiquinho 17, Barra town, T073-3258 6012, www.meusossego. com. 19 plain a/c rooms with fridges a stroll from the beach.

$ Porto da Barra, R Beira Mar, T073-3258 6349, www.pousadaportodabarra.com. Family-run *pousada* right on the beach with simple concrete and tile a/c rooms in long annexes. The best are on the upper floor. Decent breakfast. Friendly owner.

Itacaré p60

The area is becoming very popular and prices are going up all the time. Book well ahead in high season.

$$$$ Txai Resort, Praia de Itacarezinho, T073-2627 6363, www.txai.com.br. The most comfortable hotel around Itacaré, set on a deserted beach with very spacious and tastefully appointed bungalows overlooking a long, deep-blue pool shaded by its own stand of palms. Excellent spa and a full range of activities including diving and horse riding.

$$$ Art Jungle, T073-9996 2167, www. artjungle.org. A modern sculpture garden with 6 treehouses in the middle of the forest. All have views out to the sea and to the Rio de Contas. A favourite with celebrities such as Sean Penn, Jade Jagger and Gisele Bündchen.

$$$ Maria Farinha, T073-3251 3515, www.mariafarinhapousada.com.br. Simple family-run *pousada* in a concrete annexe overlooking a little pool. Pleasant *maloca*-shaped communal breakfast area, quiet and good for families. Disabled access.

$$$ Nainas, Praia da Concha, T073-3251 2683, www.nainas.com.br. Rooms in these colourful cabins and annexes are simple but comfortable, with little decks, splashes of colour from bedspreads and art and craft decor. They are set in a lush garden close to the beach.

$$$ Sage Point, Praia de Tiririca, T073-3251 2030, www.pousadasagepoint.com.br. Ocean-front *pousada* with smart wooden chalets in a tropical garden overlooking the sea, each with their own hammock-strewn terraces. Some are a little small but all have wonderful views. The Cuban owner, Ana, speaks English and can organize trips to nearby beaches.

$$$ Villa Bella, Praia da Concha, T073-3251 2985, www.pousadavillabella.com.br. A modern beach hotel with well-appointed rooms set in duplex garden cabins, decked out with wood-panel floors and sitting over a generous pool in a large lawned garden.

$$$ Villa de Ecoporan, T073-3251 2470, www.villaecoporan.com.br. Brightly coloured spacious chalets gathered around a charming little pool in a hammock-filled garden. Between the town and Praia da Concha. Good Bahian restaurant.

$$$ Vira Canoa, Praia da Concha, T073-3251 2525, www.viracanoa.com.br. Maroon bungalows overlooking a lush pool in a pretty garden. Each is decorated with arts and crafts and is filled with heavy wood furniture, plasma-screen TVs and iPod docking stations. The restaurant has good seafood and massages are available.

$$ Estrela, R Pedro Longo 34, Centro, T073-3251 2006, www.pousadaestrela.com.br. A range of well-maintained, pretty duplex chalets and bungalows with rustic wooden fittings and pastel colours on the walls. The *pousada* serves an excellent home-made breakfast with a huge choice. Staff are friendly and services include free Wi-Fi.

$$ Pousada da Lua, Praia da Concha, T073-3251 2209, http://pousadadalua.com. A handful of terracotta-tile roofed chalets, some of which are large enough for 4 people set in a forest filled with marmosets and parakeets. Great breakfast.

$$ Sítio Ilha Verde, R Ataíde Seubal 234, T073-3251 2056, www.ilhaverde.com. br. These bungalows sitting in a verdant, flower-filled garden are painted in warm tones and are stylishly decorated with local arts and crafts. The largest have space for an entire family.

$ Albergue o Pharol, Praça Santos Dumont 7, Itacaré, T073-3251 2527, www.albergueo pharol.com.br. A pleasant, well-kept hostel 10 mins' walk from the bus stop for Ilhéus in the centre of town and offering simple dorms, triples and doubles and public areas with heavy wooden furniture and lacy hammocks.

$ Pedra Bonita, R Lodonio Almeida 120, T073-3251 3037, www.itacarehostel.com.br. Pleasant little HI hostel with small doubles and dorms (cheaper) in an annexe, a small pool, internet and TV area. Friendly staff.

Camping

Tropical Camping, R Pedro Longo 187, T073-3251 3531. A small palm-shaded campsite in the centre of Itacaré town.

Ilhéus and around *p61, map p61*
There are plenty of cheap hotels in Ilhéus near the municipal *rodoviária* in centre; not all are desirable (check for hot-pillow establishments that rent rooms by the hour).

$$$$ Fazenda da Lagoa, Rodovia BA-001, Una, T073-3236 6046, www. fazendadalagoa.com.br. Carioca Lia Siqueira and Mucki Skowronski's super-chic beach bungalows offer privacy and intimate designer luxury that lures celebrities. However, the real star here is the wilderness landscape: the vast, empty beach and pounding ocean; the adjacent rainforest and mangrove wetlands; and the beautiful river and lake. Unfortunately the owners have little knowledge of natural history, so nature-lovers are advised to organize their own guides (with prior notice) through Orbitá in Ilhéus (see page 69).

$$$ Hotel Barravento, Malhado Beach, R Nossa Senhora das Graças 276, Ilhéus, T073-3634 3223, www.barravento.com.br. The smartest hotel in the city. Ask for the penthouse (there is usually no extra charge), which includes breakfast and a fridge.

$$$ Jardim Atlântico, Rodovia Ilheus-Olivenca Km 2, Jardim Atlântico, Ilhéus, T073-3632 4711, www.hotel jardimatlantico.com.br. One of Bahia's few luxurious beach hotels that not only welcomes children but provides kids' clubs, activities and a little water park. There are tennis courts, sauna, gym and activities for the adults. Rooms have their own little garden and hammock terraces and, thankfully, as the restaurant is a long way away, food is decent.

$$ Britânia, R Jorge Amado s/n, Ilhéus, T073-3634 1722, www.brasilheus.com.br/ britania_por.htm. The best value in the town centre with large rooms in an early 20th-century wooden hotel just west of the cathedral square. Safe area with lots of restaurants.

🍴 Restaurants

Tinharé and Morro de São Paulo
p57

There are plenty of restaurants in Morro de São Paulo town and on the 2nd and 3rd beaches. Most of them are okay though somewhat overpriced. For cheap eats stay in a *pousada* that includes breakfast, stock up at the supermarket and buy seafood snacks at the *barracas* on the 2nd beach.

$$ Tinharé, down a little set off steps off R Caminha de Praia, The food here bursts with flavour, especially the delicious *peixe escabeche* (fresh fish cooked in coconut milk and served in a sizzling cast-iron pot). The portions are so generous they serve 2-3.

$$-$ Sabor da Terra, R Caminho da Praia, T075-3652 1156. A very popular lunchtime per kilo and à la carte evening restaurant serving great *moquecas* and seafood.

Ilha de Boipeba *p59*
Boipeba has cheap eats in the town and surprisingly good food at the **Pousada Santa Clara** and the rustic restaurants in Moreré.
$$ Santa Clara (see Where to stay, page 65), Boipeba. San Francisco panache in rustic but elegantly decorated tropical surrounds. Come for dinner. Highly recommended.
$ Mar e Coco, Moreré, T075-3653 6013. Very fresh seafood in idyllic surroundings, shaded by coconuts and next to a gently lapping bath-warm sea.

Itacaré *p60*
There are plenty of restaurants in Itacaré, most of them on **R Lodônio Almeida**. Menus here are increasingly chic and often include a respectable wine list.
$$$ Casa Sapucaia, R Lodônio Almeida, T073-3251 3091. Sophisticated Bahian food with an international twist from 2 ex-round-the-world sailors. Try the delicious king prawn caramelized with ginger.
$$$ Dedo de Moça, R Plinio Soares 26 (next to the São Miguel church), T073-3251 3391. One of Bahia's best restaurants. The chef was trained by Vagner Aguiar, who worked at São Paulo's award-winning **Laurent** restaurant, and her menu of dishes that combine Brazilian ingredients with French and oriental techniques has been expanded by local chef Carol.
$$$ O Casarão Amarelo, Praia da Coroinha, T073-9996 0599. Swiss-owned restaurant in one of the most beautiful colonial buildings in the town. International menu which is good in parts. The fish is always a reliable choice.
$$ Beco das Flores, R Lodônio Almeida 134, T073-3251 3121. The busiest restaurant in Itacaré, serving good wood-fired pizzas in tastefully decorated surroundings to a well-dressed post-beach crowd.
$$ La In, R Lodônio Almeida 116, Centro, T073-3251 3054. Great little Bahian and seafood restaurant decorated with colourful art painted by the owner, Marcio, and serving very good-value lunches and dinners. Be sure to try the house speciality: fish in prawn sauce baked in a banana leaf.
$ O Restaurante, R Pedro Longo 150, T073-3251 2012. One of the few restaurants with a *prato feito*, alongside a mixed seafood menu.

Ilhéus and around *p61, map p61*
Specialities include the local drink, *coquinho*, coconut filled with *cachaça*, which is only for the strongest heads. There are cheap eats from the various seafood stalls on the *praça* and near the cathedral.
$$$ Vesúvio, Praça Dom Eduardo, T073-3634 4724. Next to the cathedral, made famous by Amado's novel, now Swiss-owned. Very good but pricey.
$ Acarajé de Irene, Praça Castro Alves. Great traditional *acarajé* and other Bahian snacks. Long a local favourite; people come from all over the city just to eat here.

🎵 Bars and clubs

Tinharé and Morro de São Paulo *p57*
There is always plenty going on in Morro. The liveliest bars are on the 2nd beach where you'll also find the throbbing **Pulsa** nightclub. These tend to get going after 2300 when the restaurants in town empty.

Ilha de Boipeba *p59*
Nightlife on Boipeba is limited to star-gazing or having a beer in town.

Itacaré *p60*
The liveliest bars of the moment are **Toca do Calango**, Praça dos Cachorros and **Mar e Mel** on the Praia das Conchas. The **Casarão Amarelo** restaurant becomes a dance club after 2300 on weekends. There is frequent extemporaneous *forró* and other live music all over the city and most restaurants and bars have some kind of music Oct-Apr.

❶ What to do

Tinharé and Morro de São Paulo
p57
Tour operators
There are numerous little agencies offering
boat, beach and snorkelling tours around
Morro and it's an idea to shop around for
the best price. They include **Puro Prazer**,
T075-8176 8038, www.lanchaspuroprazer.
com.br, and a cooperative of taxi drivers and
operators based at Receptivo (just behind
the 2nd Beach) who run tours to Gamboa
(US$15), Garapoa village and beach (one of
the island's prettiest, US$25) and day trips to
Boipeba (US$35). All prices are per person.

Peninsula de Maraú *p59*
Maris, T073-3255 2348, www.lagoado
cassange.com.br. Boat trips around the Baía
de Camamu (including to the Tremembé
waterfalls and to the surrounding islands),
trekking along the beaches (including a
wonderful 2-day walk between the Praia do
Pontal and the Rio Piracanga) and trips to
small, traditional fishing villages such as the
boat-building community of Cajaíba.

Ilhéus and around *p61, map p61*
Tour operators
Orbitá, R Marquês de Paranaguá 270,
T073-3634 7700, www.orbitaexpedicoes.
com.br. Organizes adventure trips, visits to
Maraú and general tours. The guides are
excellent and knowledgeable. The company
also operates out of both Itacaré and Una
on a pre-arranged pick-up scheme. Transfers
can be arranged to **Fazenda da Lagoa** and
throughout Bahia as far as the Chapada
Diamantina.

❷ Transport

Tinharé and Morro de São Paulo
p57
Details on current flights and ferry times to
Morro de São Paulo can be found on www.
morrodesaopaulobrasil.com.br.

Air There are several daily direct flights
from the 3rd beach at Morro de São Paulo
to Salvador. These cost US$120-130 one
way. Times vary seasonally and from
year to year but are usually as follows:
Salvador–Morro (0830, 1230, 1500, 1530),
Morro–Salvador (0915, 1315, 1600, 1615).
For further details ask your hotel to contact
Addey, T071-3377 1393, www.addey.
com.br, **Aerostar**, T071-3377 4406, www.
aerostar. com.br, or drop into the airport
office next to the landing strip on Morro.

Ferry Several companies run catamarans
from Morro de São Paulo to the Terminal
Marítimo in front of the Mercado Modelo in
Salvador (1½-2 hrs). Times vary according to
the weather but there are usually several a
day 0800-1400; check with the tourist office
or **Catamarã Gamboa do Morro**, T071-9975
6395. There are also water taxis.
  Boats from Morro de São Paulo and
Gamboa run to the main bridge in **Valença**
(1½ hrs) 5 times a day, US$2.50 (see under
Valença, above). There is also a *lancha
rápida* which takes 25 mins and costs US$8.
Private boat hire can also be arranged;
contact **Jario**, T075-3741 1681, or book
through your *pousada*.

Morro via Valença
Bus Long-distance buses run from the
new *rodoviária* on Av Maçônica. Many
buses a day to **Salvador**, 5 hrs, US$6,
several companies, including **Aguia Branca**,
T075-3450 4400. **São Jorge** to **Itabuna**,
5 hrs, US$5, very slow. For the shortest
route to Salvador, take a bus via Nazaré das
Farinhas to Bom Despacho (130 km), and
take a ferry from there to the São Joaquim
ferry terminal. To **Bom Despacho** on
Itaparica, Camarujipe and Águia Branca
companies, 16 a day, 1 hr 45 mins, US$3.60.

Ferry There are boats to **Gamboa** (1½ hrs)
and **Morro de São Paulo** (1½ hrs) from
the main bridge in Valença, 5 times a day
(signalled by a loud whistle). The fare is

US$2.50. The *lancha rápida* takes 25 mins and costs US$8. Only Salvador–Valença buses leaving 0530-1100 connect with ferries. If not stopping in Valença, get out of the bus by the main bridge in town, don't wait until you get to the *rodoviária*, which is a long way from the ferry. Private boat hire can be arranged if you miss the ferry schedule. A responsible local boatman is Jario, T075-3741 1681; he can be contacted to meet travellers arriving at the *rodoviária* for transfer to Morro. He also offers excursions to other islands, especially **Boipeba**. There is a regular boat from Valença to Boipeba on weekdays 1000-1230 depending on tide, return 1500-1700, 3-4 hrs.

Ilha de Boipeba *p59*

Boat Day-trips to the island run from Morro de São Paulo (see page 58). There is a regular boat from Boipeba to **Valença** on weekdays 1500-1700, 3-4 hrs. Overnight excursions to the village are possible. Contact **Zé Balacha**, T075-9148 0343, or book through your *pousada*.

Barra Grande and the Peninsula de Maraú *p59*

Air There are scheduled air taxis from the airport at Barra Grande to **Morro de São Paulo** and **Salvador**.

Boat Boats run from Barra Grande to **Camamu** several times a day Oct-Mar and once daily year round (boats: 1 hr, US$3; *lancha*: 20 mins, US$15).

Itacaré *p60*

Bus Frequent buses to **Ilhéus** (the nearest town with an airport), 45 mins, US$7 along the newly paved road. To **Salvador**, change at **Ubaitaba** (3 hrs, US$3), Ubaitaba–Salvador, 6 hrs, US$12, several daily.

Ilhéus and around *p61, map p61*

Air A taxi from town to the airport costs US$8. There are flights to **Salvador**, **Belo Horizonte**, **São Paulo**, **Brasília**, **Curitiba**, **Porto Seguro** and **Rio de Janeiro** with GOL, www.voegol.com.br, TAM, www.tam.com.br, and Webjet, www.webjet.com.br. Services are often cut back in low season.

Bus and boat Most long-distance buses leave from the *rodoviária*, 4 km from town. However, the **Itabuna–Olivença** bus goes through the centre of Ilhéus. Several buses run daily to **Salvador**, 7 hrs, US$30 (*leito* US$45, Expresso São Jorge), the 0620 bus goes via **Itaparica**, leaving passengers at Bom Despacho ferry station on the island (from where it is a 50-min ferry to **Salvador**). To Itacaré, 45 mins-1 hr, US$8. To **Eunápolis**, 4 hrs, US$25, this bus also leaves from the central bus terminal. Local buses leave from Praça Cairu.

ⓘ Directory

Tinharé and Morro de São Paulo *p57*

Banks There are no banks on the island, but there are Bradesco and Banco do Brasil ATMs in the town and cash dollars can be exchanged in *casas de câmbio* in the village.
Internet There are several internet cafés.

Itacaré *p60*

Banks and internet Theres a Bradesco ATM in the Praça do Forum and a branch of Banco do Brasil at R 31 Março, T073-3251 2212, with a Visa ATM. The town has the usual plethora of internet cafés.

Ilhéus and around *p61, map p100*

Banks Bradesco, R Marquês de Paranaguá 8, T073-3234 5233 will change money and have Visa ATMs.

Discovery and Whale coasts

The beaches of the far south of Bahia are among the finest in Brazil: long strands of fine white sand washed by bath-warm sea, or pounded by bottle-green surf and backed by swaying rows of coconut palms. Some are remote and completely deserted, others are watched over by busy resorts and party towns like Porto Seguro and Arraial d'Ajuda, or forgotten little villages like Caraíva, Corumbau and Curumuxatiba with only a handful of simple *pousadas*. Pretty Trancoso is perhaps the chicest beach destination north of Punta del Este in Uruguay, with a ream of gorgeous beach boutiques of the kind that grace the pages of Departures magazine or Taschen coffee-table books. Offshore, in the far south, are the Abrolhos: an archipelago of rocky coral islands fringed with reef. The islands form part of one of Brazil's most carefully protected marine reserves and are one of the best places in South America for seeing humpback whales. Back on the mainland, Bahia's far south is dotted with indigenous Pataxó villages and has extensive areas of Mata Atlântica rainforest. This area, around the pyramidal mountain at Monte Paschoal, is under threat from eucalyptus plantations used to produce toilet paper.

The Discovery Coast takes its name from the first landing by the Portuguese. In AD 1500, Pedro Álvares Cabral became the first European to see Brazil, sighting land at Monte Pascoal south of Porto Seguro. The sea here was too open to offer a safe harbour, so Cabral sailed his fleet north, entering the mouth of the Rio Burnahém to find the harbour he later called 'Porto Seguro' (safe port).

Porto Seguro → *For listings, see pages 81-88. Phone code: 073. Population: 140,000.*

Modern Porto Seguro is rapidly developing into southern Bahia's largest and most cosmopolitan coastal city, with residents from all over the world. Located on the Rio Buranhém, which separates the city from Arraial across the water, the attractive dockland area retains a handful of pretty colonial houses.

On the hill above is the higgledy-piggledy **Centro Histórico**, a peaceful place spread out on a grassy slope, with lovely gardens and panoramic views. Brazil began here – on the far side of the grassy square is a block of Cantabrian marble engraved with the Cross Of The Order Of Christ and marking the spot where the conquistador Gonçalo Coelho formally took the Discovery Coast (and by extension the country) from the Tupiniquim people in 1503. Brazil's oldest church sits behind: the **Nossa Senhora da Misericórdia** ① *Praça Pero de Campos Tourinho, T073-3288 5182, Sat-Wed 0930-1330 and 1430-1700, free*, a squat, functional little building in paintbox blue, built in 1526, with heavy fortified walls and a little scrolled Rococo pediment added like a cake decoration. Nearby, and sitting in the ruins of a monastery ransacked by the ancestors of the modern Pataxó, is the Jesuit church of **São Benedito** ① *R Dr Antônio Ricaldi s/n*, built in 1549 with even more heavily fortified walls and the church of **Nossa Senhora da Pena** ① *Praça Pero de Campos Tourinho s/n, T073-3288 6363, daily 0900-1200 and 1400-1700, free*, dating from 1708, but built over another fortified 16th-century structure. Inside is what is said to be the oldest statue in Brazil – an undistinguished effigy of St Francis of Assisi. Next door is the sacred art museum and former jail – the handsome 18th-century **Casa de Câmara e Cadêia** ① *Praça Pero de Campos Tourinho s/n, T073-3288 5182, daily 0900-1700, free*.

Arriving in Porto Seguro

Getting there Aeroporto de Porto Seguro ① *Estrada do Aeroporto s/n, 2 km north of town, T073-3288 1880*, has connections with Rio de Janeiro, São Paulo, Belo Horizonte, Ilhéus, Salvador, Porto Alegre, Brasília, Curitiba and Vitória. There are banks and a car rental booth in the terminal. A taxi to the centre costs US$8. The **rodoviária** ① *2 km west of the centre, on the road to*

Porto Seguro

CIDADE HISTÓRICA

Farol
NS da Pena
NS da Misericórdia
Gonçalo Coelho
Praça Pero de Campos Tourinho
Gonçalo Coelho Monument
NS do Rosário
Av Beira Mar BR-367
Praia do Cruzeiro
To Santa Cruz de Cabrália

To Airport
To ⑩

Av dos Navegantes
R 15 de Novembro
R Mal Deodoro da Fonseca
R Cova da Moça
R da Faca
AV 22 de Abril
Banco do Brasil
R do Golfo
R do Cajueiro
R Pero Vaz de Caminha
R Antônio Osório
R Getúlio Vargas
M Batista
R Z de Julho
R São Pedro
R P Cabral
R Assis Chateaubriand
Praça Inaiá
NS do Brasil
Bradesco
Praça Visconde de Porte Seguro
Praça da Bandeira
Praça dos Pataxós
Rio Buranhém

To Arraial da Ajuda (5 minutes)

N

100 metres
100 yards

Where to stay
Albergue Porto Seguro 7
Estalagem Porto Seguro 1

La Torre 11
Navegantes 2
Pousada dos Raizes 6
Solar da Praça 4
Solar do Imperador 10
Vela Branca 5
Xurupita 12

Eunápolis, receives direct buses from Ilhéus, Salvador, São Paulo and Rio de Janeiro (direct bus at 1600). Other buses go via via Eunápolis, which has connections with Porto Seguro every 30 minutes (US$5, one hour). The *rodoviária* has cafés and snack bars. Taxis charge US$6 to the town or ferry (negotiate at quiet times). ▸▸ *See Transport, page 86.*

Getting around Buses run from the waterfront to the old *rodoviária* near the port every 30 minutes, US$0.50. Regular buses run along the seafront from Praça dos Pataxós to the northern beaches, or take a bus to Porto Belo or Santa Cruz Cabrália from the port. For beaches south of the Rio Buranhém, see Arraial d'Ajuda (below) and points further south.

Tourist Information The tourist office, **Secretária de Turismo de Porto Seguro** ① *R Pero Vaz de Caminha 475, Centro, T073-3288 3708, www.portosegurotur.com.br*, has information on tours. Alternatively, contact **Portomondo**, www.portomondo.com. ▸▸ *See What to do, page 86.*

Around Porto Seguro

North of Porto Seguro → *For listings, see pages 81-88.*

Heading north of town, on the BR-367 to Santa Cruz Cabrália (known as Avenida Beira Mar), is Bahia's second most popular tourist area, with a series of hotels and beaches. The best beaches are **Itacimirim**, **Curuípe**, **Mundaí** and **Taperapuã**, which have some lively *barracas*. The biggest (and busiest) are **Barra Point**, **Toá Toa**, **Axé Moi**, **Vira Sol** and **Barramares**. The latter are mainly Brazilian package-tour destinations and offer jet-ski hire and other watersports facilities.

A few kilometres before Cabrália, a tourist village, **Coroa Vermelha**, has sprouted at the site of Cabral's first landfall and a cross marks the spot where the first Mass was celebrated. It has a rather uncoordinated array of beach bars, hotels, rental houses and souvenir shops selling indigenous Pataxó items. Buses from Porto Seguro take about 20 minutes.

Santa Cruz Cabrália → *Phone code: 073.*
About 10 minutes north of Coroa Vermelha (25 km north of Porto Seguro), Santa Cruz Cabrália is a delightful small town at the mouth of the Rio João de Tiba. It has a lovely beach, river port, and a 450-year-old church with a fine view. It is believed to be

The Pataxó

"This is our land. You have to respect the land you are walking on because it is ours. When you arrived here this land was already ours. And what did you do to us? You stopped our progress with riot squads, gunfire and tear gas. With our blood we commemorate once more the Discovery of Brazil". (Pataxó indigenous leader during the response to the celebration of Brazil's discovery in 2000.)

The Pataxó are descendants of the Gê speaking warrior tribes who lived in the mountains along the Bahian coast, and who inflicted the heaviest defeats on the Bahian Portuguese in the first years of the colony. Since contact was made the tribe have suffered greatly. The greatest destruction was in 1951 when one of the most important villages was, ostensibly, caught in a gun battle between bandits and police. Hundreds of Pataxó, including women and children, were murdered. The Pataxó had long been campaigning to have their tribal lands in the Monte Pascoal national park returned to them. The battle was part of a concerted and ongoing effort to rid the Pataxó of their ancestral lands. In 1961 the federal government converted 22,500 ha of land traditionally occupied by the Pataxó into the Monte Pascoal National Park. The Pataxó were violently evicted. Much of their territory was later ceded to big landowners for farming cacau and planting eucalyptus. On 19 August 1999, numerous indigenous Pataxó people set up camp at the national park, declaring that 'Monte Pascoal belongs to the Pataxó' and demanding the transformation of

'what the authorities call Monte Pascoal National Park into an indigenous park, the land of the Pataxó, to preserve it and to rehabilitate it'. Another Pataxó group, the Pataxó Hã-Hã-Hãe were treated equally badly. By the 1970s they had been shunted around from one piece of land to another as successive farmers and land speculators moved into the area, eventually settling on the São Lucas ranch where they were denied proper access to drinking water and consistently persecuted. Whilst prospects remain bleak for the Pataxó they continue to fight to preserve their cultural identity. In the new millennium, two remarkable Pataxó sisters began a cultural renovation project in their village of Jaqueira. They re-introduced the Pataxó language, traditional agricultural methods and implemented an ecotourism project to provide income for the community. Young Pataxó people have found new pride in their culture rather than leaving the community. The journalist Aricema Pataxó of the University of Bahia publishes a blog on the Pataxó (http://aricemaindiosdabahia. blogspot.com). A visit to Jaqueira is one of the highlights of a journey through southern Bahia (see page 75). The Pataxó continue to lobby for the right to live on their ancestral lands. The World Rainforest Movement have details on their latest effort (www. wrm.org.uy) and provide international support for their campaign. For further information see http://pib.socioambiental. org/en/povo/pataxo-ha-ha-hae, http:// www.indiosonline.org.br/novo.

the site of the first landing in Brazil by the Portuguese explorer Pedro Álvares Cabral in 1500. A good trip from here is to **Coroa Alta**, a reef 50 minutes away by boat. It passes along the tranquil river to the reef with crystal waters and good snorkelling. There is a daily departure at 1000. A recommended boatman is **Zezé** (T073-3282 1152), who can usually be found on the square by the river's edge; he is helpful and knowledgeable. The trip costs around US$25 without lunch.

A 15-minute river crossing by ferry to a new road on the opposite bank gives easy access to the deserted beaches of **Santo André** and **Santo Antônio**. As yet, few tourists make it to here, but the new road is certain to change this. Hourly buses run between Santa Cruz and Porto Seguro (23 km).

Estação Veracel Veracruz
ⓘ *Rodovia BR-367 Km 37, T073-3166 1535/8802 0161, www.veracel.com.br/veracruz, pre-booking necessary for visits Tue and Thu 0830-1630 and Sat 0830-1130.*
This 6000-ha private reserve, halfway between Santa Cruz Cabrália and Porto Seguro, is one of the best locations in southern Bahia for wildlife- and birdwatching. There are some 307 species of birds (with 21 threatened or endangered species and 32 endemics) and 40 mammals (including tapir, jaguar, thin-spined arboreal porcupine, brown howler monkey, Geoffroy's marmoset, crested capuchin and coastal black-handed titi monkey). There are scores of reptiles and amphibians and birdwatching is excellent, with rare species such as the red-billed curassow and banded and white-winged cotingas. This is one of the few locations outside the Amazon where Harpy eagles are known to nest. Specialist birding tours are available with **Ciro Albano** (see What to do, page 86).

Jaqueira Pataxó village
Some 8 km north of Porto Seguro, the beautiful and inspiring *Pataxó* indigenous reserve of Jaqueira is well worth a visit. Its traditional houses lie in the heart of a stand of indigenous-owned rainforest. All the food is either grown or hunted using traditional techniques. And a small craft shop selling beautiful ceramics, sacred incense and art provides extra revenue. The project was conceived by two impressive *Pataxó* sisters who despaired at the loss of *Pataxó* culture in the villages of southern Bahia. Their ecotourism and cultural recuperation model has completely rejuvenated *Pataxó* culture. Young people are speaking their own language again and rediscovering their identity. It is possible to visit or even stay in the village. Trips can be organized with **Portomondo**, www.portomondo.com, which works closely with the *Pataxó*. For further information visit www.rabarsa.com/pataxo.

South of Porto Seguro → *For listings, see pages 81-88.*

Arraial da Ajuda → *Phone code: 073.*
A five-minute float across the Rio Buranhém from the docks at Porto Seguro brings you to Arraial da Ajuda, a pretty little colonial village-turned-beach-party town and a more popular base for travellers than Porto. Arraial is an ideal place to get stuck, with a string of gorgeous beaches that begin at the mouth of the river at **Araçaipe** and continue south indefinitely. The little hotels behind the sand are on a far smaller scale than Porto's package-tourist towers and cater to shallow as well as deep pockets. The town itself has a string of pleasant little bars and restaurants; all of which are easily manageable on foot. Arraial is also one of the best places in Brazil to learn capoeira. At Brazilian holiday times (especially New Year and Carnaval) it is very crowded, almost to bursting point.

The town centre is clustered around the pretty 16th-century church of **Nossa Senhora da Ajuda** (1549), which sits high on a cliff, affording great views of the palm-covered coast. The principal streets extend off the square in front of the church. The largest, which is lined with shops, bars, restaurants and *pousadas*, is called Broadway. There's a party here or on one of the beaches almost every night in high season.

Arraial's beaches are splendid: some pounded by surf, others are little bays gently lapped by an Atlantic tamed by an offshore reef. Most have *barracas* selling good simple seafood and chilled drinks, and playing music. From north to south they are as follows. **Araçaípe** is popular with families and day-visitors from Porto, and has several pretty beach hotels and *pousadas*. **D'Ajuda** is in front of the town and has a small protected area. **Mucugê** just to the south of town, has good surf, plenty of beach *barracas* for *forró* and lambada parties in the summer. To reach these, take Rua da Praia out of town. South beyond Mucugê is **Parracho**, which is popular for windsurfing and kayaking (rental available); followed by **Pitinga**, with strong waves breaking on the offshore reef creating some decent surf. The penultimate beach is **Lagoa Azul**, backed by cliffs, with gorgeous sand and strong surf. Few make it to the beach farthest south, **Taipé**, an hour's walk from Arraial. It is backed by sandstone cliffs and has glassy water and a handful of *barracas*. At low tide it is possible to walk to from Taipé to Trancoso (see below) along the beach via the village of **Rio da Barra**; allow two hours. A dirt road behind the beach follows the same route and is plied by taxis and cars; it is easy to hitch a lift.

Arraial da Ajuda

To 2 3 4 11 & Ferry to Porto Seguro

To Praia Araçaípe

Est Arraial Trancoso

R do Campo

Manuel A dos Santos

Ladeira de Santa

Estrada de Arraial

Praia D'Ajuda

1

4 Praça São Brás

Praça Brig Eduardo Gomes

Nossa Senhora da Ajuda

Broadway

R FM Nobre

Fonte Sagrada

8

R São João

R 7 de Capoeira

R CA Parracho

Beco do Jeque

2

R 5 Antônio

R Vista Alegre

Trav S Antônio

6

R do Ipê

R Jequitibá

Alam dos Flamboyants

Alam dos Oitis

5

1

8

Praia Mucugê

Est do Mucugê

Est Alto do Mucugê

Est da Pitinga

To 9, Praia Parracho, Praia Pitinga, Lagoa Azul & Taipé

N

100 metres

100 yards

Where to stay
Arraial Hostel 1
Camping do Caju 2
Pousada Canto d'Alvorada 3
Pousada do Roballo 5
Pousada Erva Doce 6

Pousada Mar Aberto 8
Pousada Pitinga 9
Quinta do Porto 4
Sole Mio 11

Restaurants
Don Fabrizio 1

Manguti 2
Paulo Pescador 4
Rosa dos Ventos 8

Arriving in Arraial da Ajuda Ferries from Porto Seguro run across the Rio Buranhém to the south bank every 30 minutes day and night (three minutes, US$0.60 for foot passengers, US$5 for cars). From there, it is a further 5 km to Arraial da Ajuda town centre (US$1 by bus, *combis* charge US$1.50 per person, taxis US$5), although the first *pousadas* are literally on the Arraial riverbank. It is not necessary to return to Porto Seguro to venture into the rest of Bahia. Arraial is connected by bus to Eunápolis and Caraíva, and Trancoso to the south. Various agencies in town offer transfers by buggy or Land Rover to Corumbau all the way to Abrolhos. **Portomondo** (see What to do, page 86) is by far the best and most reliable.

Trancoso → *Phone code: 073.*

In the last five years this once-sleepy little village, 15 km south of Arraial, has become Bahia's chicest beach destination, beloved of the Brazilian and international jet-set for its combination of low-key atmosphere and high-fashion labels. The coolest São Paulo names fill the tiny shopping centre and the town and beaches are dotted with smart designer boutiques and haute-rural restaurants offering the best food outside Rio de Janeiro and São Paulo. Celebrities come here to be recognized only by those they wish to be recognized by, especially the Mario Testino set. Despite its status, Trancoso remains a simple little town at heart, and herein lies its charm. It is glossy but intimate, with life focusing on the **Quadrado**, a long grassy square where locals play football in the evening. The square is crowned with the little whitewashed 17th-century church of **São João Batista**, and lined with colourful little *casas*, each housing a bikini boutique, crafts shop, fashionable restaurant, bar or guesthouse. The houses are particularly enchanting at night, when they contrast with the dark indigo canvas of the rainforest, under a dome of stars.

Below the Quadrado are a stretch of beaches extending away to the north and south. The most famous and the closest to town are **Praia do Trancoso** and **Praia dos Nativos**, both washed by gentle waves, with coral far offshore and a cluster of chic-shack *barracas* that host parties for the designer-label brigade during the summer months. **Coqueiros**, across the little river to the north is quieter, with one simple restaurant and a view. To the south beyond Trancoso beach are **Rio Verde**, with a little river, and beyond it **Itapororoca** a deserted beach with just a few very expensive houses and good clear-water snorkelling.

Arriving in Trancoso In high season, *combis* ply the dirt road along the coast between Arraial and Trancoso, leaving when full. Buses run along the newly paved road between Porto Seguro, Arraial da Ajuda and Trancoso at least once an hour in high season (US$3 from Porto Seguro, US$2 from Arraial). There are two daily buses from Caraíva; with an extra bus in high season. Taxis from Arraial cost around US$30; from Porto airport US$40-50. Like any of the Bahian resorts, it is also possible to organize air taxis from Rio or São Paulo or helicopter transfers from Arraial, Caraíva and Corumbau (see **Portomondo**, page 86, for details). Trancoso can be packed out in high season. Be sure to book ahead. There are no really cheap rooms. Various tour operators around the main square sell *combi*, bus and air tickets for destinations throughout Bahia and organize day trips to Espelho and beyond. The easiest way to get around town is by bike, on foot or motorbike taxi.

Espelho

A 50-minute drive along the dirt road to Caraíva, Espelho is one of the state's most beautiful beaches: a glassy bay fringed with white sand and rocks with a handful of very plush beach hotels and a delightful restaurant. The Caraíva bus will drop you at the turn off to the beach, from where it is a 5-km walk; or visit as part of a tour.

Caraíva → *Phone code: 073.*

This incredibly peaceful, atmospheric fishing town, 65 km south of Porto Seguro, is on the banks of the Rio Caraíva. Electricity (during the daytime only) and hot water were only installed in 2008 and the streets are sand so there are no cars. The marvellous beaches here make a real escape from Trancoso, Arraial and Porto Seguro. Despite difficult access, Caraíva is becoming increasingly popular.

There is a good walk north to **Praia do Satu** (where Señor Satu provides an endless supply of coconut milk), or 6 km south to a rather sad Pataxó indigenous village; watch the tides as you may get cut off. Horses can be hired through any of the *pousadas* and buggy rides to Corumbau (from where buses connect to Cumuruxatiba) can be organized from the town square with the Pataxó (US$40). Or you can walk the 12 km along the beach to the river that separates Caraíva's last beach with Corumbau village; there is a boatman here for crossings (US$2, 10 minutes). Boats can be hired (US$50 per day) at the river port in Caraíva for excursions to Caruípe Beach, Espelho, snorkelling at Pedra de Tatuaçu reef or Corombau (take your own mask and fins), or for trips up the beautiful river Rio Caraíva which gets into wild, pristine rainforest some 10 km inland. **Prainha** river beach, about 30 minutes away, and mangrove swamps can also be visited by canoe or launch.

Arriving in Caraíva Caraíva is connected to Trancoso by two daily buses (three in high season), along a very poor dirt road. The journey involves a river crossing and can take as long as three hours in the wet season (April to June). If arriving by bus from the south, change in Itabela (departs at 1500), or take a taxi; about 50 km. The high season is December to February and July. There are plenty of cheap *pousadas* and restaurants along the rustic sandy streets. Most bars have live *forró* in the summer. Flip-flops are best for walking along the sand streets, and take a torch as it is very dark at night.

Parque Nacional de Monte Pascoal
ⓘ *16 km north of Itamaraju, Caixa Postal 076, CEP 45830-000, Itamaraju, T073-3281 2419.*
The national park was set up in 1961 to preserve the flora, fauna and birdlife of the coast where Europeans first landed in Brazil. There is a bus from Itamaraju at 0600 (Monday to Friday); taxis run from Itamaraju cost around US$50 for the round trip including waiting time. Or the park can be visited with a tour group such as **Portomondo**, see page 86.

Corumbau
This tiny fishing village sits on a little promontory of land that sticks out into the deep blue of the Bahian Atlantic. It's a one-beach buggy town, with a tiny church and a handful of very cheap *pousadas* and restaurants; but it is fringed with beaches every bit as gorgeous as any of those around Caraíva or Trancoso. There is great snorkelling from the beach to the south of town. Foreigners are few and far between, except for a handful who come to stay at the exclusive and beautifully designed resorts to the south of the town.

Arriving in Corumbau Corumbau is not easy to reach. The best way is to organize a transfer with an agency like **Portomondo** (see page 86). However, it is possible to get here by catching the bus to Caraíva and then either sharing a buggy ride from the main square (US$40) or walking the 12 km to the river and catching the ferry boat (see above). There is one daily bus from Itamaraju.

Capoeira

Capoeira is the most visually spectacular and gymnastic of all martial arts and the only one to have originated in the Americas. Salvador is the capoeira centre of Brazil and seeing a fight between good Bahian capoeristas is an unforgettable experience. Fighters spin around each other in mock combat, never touching but performing a series of lunges, kicks and punches with dizzying speed and precision. Some wear razor blades on their feet. A ring or *roda* of other capoeristas watches, clapping, singing and beating time on a *berimbau* and hand-held drum. Every now and then they exchange places with the fighters in the centre of the ring.

Although many claim that capoeira derives from an Angolan foot-fighting ritual, this is incorrect. Capoeira originated in Brazil and there is strong evidence to suggest that it was invented by indigenous Brazilians. Padre José de Anchieta a 16th-century ethnologist makes an aside in his 1595 book *The Tupi Guarani Language* that the 'Indians amuse themselves by playing capoiera' and other Portuguese explorers like Martim de Souza recall the same. The word capoeira itself comes from Tupi-Guarani and means 'cleared forest' and the postures, including many of the kicks, spins and the crouching position taken by those in the circle are all Brazilian-Indian. It was in indigenous capoeiras that the fight was passed on to African plantation slaves who modified them, added African chants and rhythms and the *berimbau*; an instrument probably brought to Brazil from West Africa. The art was used as a weapon against the soldiers of the enslaved African king Zumbi who established the Americas' only free slave state just north of Bahia in the 1700s.

Caravelas → *Phone code: 073.*

Continuing south, Caravelas is a charming little town on the banks of the Caravelas estuary, surrounded by mangroves. There are eight fine white-sand beaches nearby. The town is well known for its Catholic festivals, which attract thousands of pilgrims. Caravelas was a major trading port in the 17th and 18th centuries and the town's name was taken from the Portuguese sailing boats whose technology opened up the world to Lisbon. It is now slowly developing as a resort for Brazilian tourism. The best beaches are about 10 km away at the fishing village of **Barra de Caravelas** (hourly buses). There is a helpful tourist information, **Ibama Centro de Visitantes** ⓘ *Barão do Rio Branco 281.*

Arriving in Caravelas Caravelas is 36 km south of Prado on the BA-001, on the banks of the Rio Caravelas and is served by frequent buses from Eunápolis and Itamaraju from where there are connections to the rest of the state. There are two weekly buses from Porto Seguro and daily connections to Prado to the north. The town is the departure point for the Abrolhos Islands.

Parque Nacional Marinho dos Abrolhos

Abrolhos is an abbreviation of *Abre os olhos*, 'Open your eyes', from Amérigo Vespucci's exclamation when he first sighted the reef in 1503. Established in 1983, the park consists of five small islands: **Redonda**, **Siriba**, **Guarita**, **Sueste** and **Santa Bárbara**, which are volcanic in origin. There are also abundant coral reefs and good diving. Darwin visited the archipelago in 1830 and Jacques Cousteau studied the marine environment here.

The archipelago national park protects the most extensive coral reefs in the south Atlantic with four times as many endemic species than the reefs and atolls in the Caribbean. There are numerous endemic species, including giant brain corals, crustaceans and molluscs, as well as marine turtles and mammals threatened by extinction and huge colonies of nesting seabirds. In addition, the seas around the islands are one of the most important south Atlantic nurseries for humpback whales – which can always be seen in season.

In 2002, the Abrolhos region was declared an area of Extreme Biological Importance by the Brazilian Ministry of Environment, based on the Brazilian commitment to the international Convention on Biodiversity. For more information see **Conservation International**, www.conservation.org. The archipelago is administered by **Ibama** and a navy detachment mans a lighthouse on Santa Bárbara, which is the only island that may be visited. Visitors are not allowed to spend the night on the islands, but may stay overnight on schooners.

Arriving in the Parque Nacional Marinho dos Abrolhos The Parque Nacional Marinho dos Abrolhos is 70 km east of Caravelas. The journey to the islands takes three to four hours depending on the sea conditions. Between July and early December, humpback whale sightings are almost guaranteed. Boats leave at 0700 from the Marina Porto Abrolhos some 5 km north of Caravelas town centre (around US$50 depending on numbers) and they return at dusk. It is possible to dive or snorkel at Abrolhos. If you are coming from Porto Seguro everything including transfers and accommodation in Caravelas can be arranged by **Portomondo** ① *T073-3575 3686, www.portomondo.com*. In Caravelas, book with **Abrolhos Turismo**, or **Catamarã Veleiro Sanuk** (see page 86), through any of the hotels listed above; or directly at the Marina Porto Abrolhos. For further information see www.ilhasdeabrolhos.com.br.

Discovery and Whale coasts listings

For hotel and restaurant price codes and other relevant information, see pages 8-11.

⊜ Where to stay

Porto Seguro *p72, map p72*
Prices rise steeply Dec-Feb and Jul. Off-season rates can drop by 50%, negotiate the rate for stays of more than 3 nights. Room capacity is greater than that of Salvador. Outside Dec-Feb, rooms with bath and hot water can be rented for about US$150 per month.

There are no hotels of character on the beach; all are huge, brash affairs that look like they belong in 1970s Benidorm. The best beach boutiques are in Trancoso or Arraial, but Porto is better value than either if you opt to stay in town.

$$$$ La Torre, Av Beira Mar 9999, Praia do Mutá, T073-2105 1700, www.resortlatorre. com. One of the best big beach resorts in Porto, close to the barraca action on the thronging Praia Mutá. Rooms range from spacious family suites with sea views to boxier options for 2. There's restaurant (low-lit for courting couples in the evening) and a big, sculpted pool. Cheapest rates are through the internet and are inclusive of meals, drinks (only Brazilian alcoholic drinks are provided) and sport activities. The hotel provides enterntainment for adults and children, from light tree-top and zip line adventures and organized play times to ultralight scenic flights and scuba diving. Facilities include a sauna, gym, tennis courts and volleyball, together with regular free transfer to your barraca at the beach, and to the airport.

$$$$ Xurupita, Rua B 25, Taperapuã, T073-2105 9500, www.xurupita.com. This is one of the few Porto Seguro resort hotels which doesn't feel like a brash 1970s throwback. Annexes of plain, rooms given splashes of colour from big floral murals and furnished with dull catalogue furniture sit on a shady lawn surrounded by lush Atlantic coastal rainforest. Some have views out over the coast (which is just over 1 km away). The hotel runs transfers to the beach and into town and has a pool, restaurant and a sports centre with gym coaching, squash and tennis.

$$ Albergue Porto Seguro, R Cova da Moça 720, T073-3288 1742, www. porto segurohostel.com.br. HI hostel. Cheaper prices per person in dorms. Smart little hostel in the centre, with internet, excursions and discount rates at their sister beach hostel on Praia Taberapuan north of town.

$$ Estalagem Porto Seguro, R Mcal Deodoro 66, T073-3288 2095, www.hotel estalagem.com.br. Terraced rooms in a deep blue colonial house in the town centre. Great atmosphere and a stroll from nearby restaurants. The hotel can help with tours and transfers.

$$ Hotel Navegantes, Av 22 de Abril 212, T073-3288 2390, www.portonet.com.br/ navegantes. Simple, plain white wall and tile floor a/c rooms, with en suites and TVs, crowding over a little pool and concrete deck in the centre of town.

$$ Pousada dos Raizes, Praça dos Pataxós 196, T073-3288 4717, pousadaraizes@ hotmail.com.br. Well-kept unpretentious city hotel with helpful staff. Cheaper without breakfast. Recommended.

$$ Solar da Praça, R Assis Chateaubriand 75, Passarela do Álcool, Centro, T073-3288 2585, www.pousadasolardapraca.com. Pretty little renovated colonial townhouse with a range of basic but well-kept rooms dominated by a bed. Some with a/c and en suites in an adjacent annexe. Opt for those on the upper floors as they are less musty. The staff can organize excursions.

$$ Solar do Imperador, Estr do Aeroporto, T073-3288 8450, www.solardoimperador. com.br. Well-appointed, spacious and modern a/c rooms with en suites and balconies in a medium-sized resort hotel on the road to the airport. Large pool and wonderful views from the upper deck in the public area.

$$ Vela Branca, R Dr Antonio Ricaldi, Cidade Alta, T073-3288 2318, www. velabranca.com.br. This enormous family resort is as intimate as a shopping mall but offers cheap rates when booked through online. It's a great option for families, with kids' clubs, a kids' pool and plenty of play areas including a football pitch and a volleyball court on the beach.

Santa Cruz Cabrália *p73*
$$$$ Toca do Marlin, Estr BA-001, Km 40.5, Santo André, T073-3671 5041, www.tocado marlin.com.br. One of the most luxurious beach resorts in South America, with spacious a/c *cabañas* next to a ranch overlooking a quiet, beautiful beach some 50 km north of Porto Seguro. Excellent food and excursions.

$$$ Baía Cabrália, R Sidrack de Carvalho 141, centro, T073-3282 8000, www.baia cabralia.com.br. Medium-sized family resort with a large pool, sauna and gym.

$$ Victor Hugo, Villa de Santo André, Km 3, Santa Cruz Cabrália, T073-3671 4064, www. pousadavictorhugo.com.br. Smart, tastefully decorated little *pousada* right on the beach on the edge of an environmentally protected area.

Arraial da Ajuda *p75, map p76*
At busy times such as New Year's Eve and Carnaval, don't expect to find anything under US$15 per person in a shared room, with a minimum stay of 5-7 days.

$$$ Pousada Canto d'Alvorada, on the road to the Arraial d'Ajuda ferry, T073-3575 1218, www.cantodalvorada.com.br. Cheaper out of season. Pretty, Swiss-run *pousada* facing the beach on the edge of town with 21 cabins, a restaurant, pool, sauna and laundry facilities.

$$$ Pousada Pitinga, Praia Pitinga, T073-3575 1067, www.pousadapitinga.

com.br. Wooden chalets in a coconut-filled rainforest garden on a hill overlooking the sea. Tranquil atmosphere, great food and a pool. A member of the **Roteiros de Charme** group.

$$$ Privillage Praia, Estrada da Pitinga 1800, Praia Pitinga, T073-3575 1646, www. privillage.com.br. This tranquil *pousada* sits in secluded forest overlooking an almost deserted beach 10 mins from Arraial d'Ajuda town. Rooms are less beautiful than the setting – set in concrete chalets and with raw brick walls, tiled floors and heavy wicker furniture. All have international TV and comfortable king-sized beds and a number have ocean views. The *pousada* has a good restaurant and a pool whose waters appear to merge with the sea.

$$$ Quinta do Porto, Ponta do Apaga Fogo 1, T073-3575 1022, www.quintadoporto. com.br. Rooms in long corridors above a smart pool set in tropical gardens right on the river opposite Porto Seguro. Convenient for both Arraial and Porto towns (*combis* from Porto every 10 mins, ferries from Porto every 15 mins), and with an excellent travel agencies for onward excursions. The beach is 10-15 mins' walk.

$$ Pousada do Roballo, Estr do Mucugê, T073-3575 1053, www.pousadadoroballo. com.br. Welcoming *pousada* with a set of small rooms, each with a tiny veranda with hammock. Set in pleasant garden surroundings and with a pool.

$$ Pousada Erva Doce, Estr do Mucugê 200, T073-3575 1113, www.ervadoce.com. br. Well-appointed chalets and a decent restaurant, set in a lawned garden and with a pool.

$$ Pousada Mar Aberto, Estr do Mucugê 554, T073-3575 1153. Pretty little *pousada* with brick chalets and a pool set on the crest of a hill and set in lush gardens close to Mucugê Beach and the centre. At the lower end of the price category.

$$ Sole Mio, just off the beach road leading from the ferry to Arraial, T073-3575 1115. French owners, English spoken, laid-back with 4 chalets and an excellent pizzeria.

$ Arraial Hostel, R do Campo 94, T073-3575 1192/1998, www.arraialdajudahostel.com. br. Price per person. Smart well equipped modern backpacker hostel with IYHA discount in a large and colourful little house on the edge of town. Good facilities include a pool, bar, internet and book exchange.

Camping

Camping do Caju, T073-3575 2257, www. campingdocaju.com.br. Campsites and simple thatched roof chalets in a pretty garden surrounded by forest, just off the Estrada da Balsa (ferry road), 2 km from the centre of Arraial and 5 km from the Porto-Arraial ferry point. To get there take R Portugal from the beach where there are signposts for the campsite.

Trancoso *p77*

$$$$ Etnia, R Principal, T073-3668 1137, www.etniabrasil.com.br. This captivating eco-chic *pousada* a stroll from the Quadrado is a glossy magazine favourite, with a series of elegant and individually style bungalows gathered around a lush designer pool and set in a tropical forest garden filled with brilliantly coloured birds and butterflies. Run with *gaúcho* and Italian style, panache and efficiency.

$$$$ Mata N'ativa Pousada, Estr Velha do Arraial s/n (next to the river on the way to the beach), T073-3668 1830, www. mata nativapousada.com.br. The best in town for nature lovers and those seeking a quiet, relaxed retreat. A series of elegant and romantic cabins are set in a lovingly maintained orchid and heliconia garden with a pool by the riverside, which is a good few degrees cooler than anywhere else in Trancoso in the heat of the day. Nothing is too much trouble for the warm-hearted owners Daniel and Daniela. Both are knowledgeable about flora and fauna in the Mata Atlântica rainforest and can organize wildlife or birdwatching

excursions. Good English, Spanish and Italian spoken. Great breakfast.

$$$$ Pousada Estrela d'Água, Estrada Arraial D'Ajuda, Praia dos Nativos, T073-3668 1030, www.estreladagua.com.br. An infinity pool with waters melding into the turquoise sea leads to a light-flooded living area and a garden with luxurious faux-fishermen's cottages decorated with minimalist, clean whites and deep blues. There is free Wi-Fi throughout and the hotel follows the PNUMA UN programme for nature, installing solar power, recycling and engaging in some small welfare programmes. The bar is a favourite sunset cocktail spot.

$$$$ Villas de Trancoso, Estr Arraial D'Ajuda, T073-3668 1151, www.villasde trancoso.com. A series of luxurious cabins gathered on a lawn next to a pool and a relaxed bar and rustic wood-weight gym area on the adjacent beach. The duplex suite is perhaps the most luxurious in the town. American-run and owned and with a Californian feel. Can be hot as there isn't much shade.

$$$ Capim Santo, to the left of the main square, T073-3668 1122, www.capimsanto. com.br. Friendly, beautifully designed little *pousada* right on the edge of Quadrado and with a series of well-appointed rustic chic rooms and cabins. The restaurant is one of the best and most romantic in town. Superb breakfasts and dinners.

$$ Pousada Calypso, Parque Municipal, T073-3668 1113, www.pousadacalypso. com.br. Comfortable, spacious rooms, jacuzzis, a library and sitting area and helpful staff who speak German and English. Just off the Quadrado.

$$ Pousada Quarto Crescente, R Principal, T073-3668 1014, www. quartocrescente.net. About 500 m inland, away from the main square, on the main road to the beach. With cooking facilities, laundry and helpful owners who speak English, German, Dutch and Spanish. Map, bus times and directions on the website.

$$ Pousada Som do Mar, Beco da Praia dos Nativos, Praia dos Nativos, T073-3668 1812, www.pousadasomdomar.com.br. Simple little mock-colonial cubes with terraces hung with hammocks overlooking a tiny pool 5 mins' walk from the Nativos Beach. Internet and Wi-Fi.

$ Café Esmeralda, T073-3668 1527, www.trancosonatural.com. Tiny white-washed rooms in rather airless fan-cooled, tile-roofed bungalows right on the Quadrado. The *pousada* restaurant serves good breakfast (extra) and some of the cheapest lunches in Trancoso, and is one of the few establishments to be locally owned.

Caraíva p78

$$$ Vila do Mar, R 12 de Outubro s/n, T073-3668 5111, www.pousadaviladomar.com.br. The plushest hotel in town, with spacious, stylish airy, wooden *cabañas* overlooking the beach set on a lawn around an adult and children's pool.

$$ Pousada da Praia, Praia de Caraíva, T073-9985 4249, www.pousadapraiacaraiva.com.br. Very simple little boxes with no more than a bed, a table, chair and wardrobe. Public areas are furnished more comfortably, with an outdoor deck area hung with hammocks and dotted with wicker sofas.

$$ Pousada Flor do Mar, R 12 de Outubro s/n, on the beach, T073-9985 1608, www.caraiva.tur.br/flordomar. Charming beachfront *pousada* with airy rooms with a view – the best right next to the beach.

$$ Pousada San Antônio, Praia de Caraíva, T073-9962 2123, www.pousadasanantonio.com.br. Very simple but colourful fan-cooled rooms right on the beach and breezy public areas decorated with marine bric-a-brac and furnished with wicker chairs and hammocks.

$$ Pousada Terra, Praia de Caraíva, T073-9985 4417, www.terracaraiva.com.br. Simple cabins on the edge of the town and on the outskirts of the Monte Pascoal forest.

Camping
Camping Caraíva Praia de Caraíva, Praia de Cariava, T073-2231 4892, www.campingcaraiva.com.br. Basic but shady plots by the riverside with a communal cooking area and showers, and a selection of simple shacks with hard beds (**$**).

Corumbau p78

$$$$ Fazenda São Francisco, T011-3078 4411, www.corumbau.com.br. Spacious, well-appointed hard wood and cream cabins gathered around a pool in a palm-shaded garden 5 mins' walk from the beach.

$$$$ Vila Naia, T011-3061 1872, www.vila naia.com.br. Tastefully appointed, luxurious bungalows set in a little garden back from the beach. Very popular with fashionable Paulistanos. Intimate and romantic but not of the same standard as Tauana.

$$$ Jocotoka Village, T073-3288 2291, www.jocotoka.com.br. Brilliantly coloured, higgledy-piggledy, thatched-roof chalets grouped on a shady lawn between the beach and patchy *restinga* forest. Children under 5 and pets are not permitted.

$$$ Pousada Corumbau, T073-3573 1190, www.corumbau.tur.br. It's difficult to miss this big red 2-storey house in tiny Corumbau. There are a range of rooms – from simple concrete huts (with space for up to 4 at a push), to big tiled rooms in the main building. All are homey but decorated in brash colours.

$ Vila Pousada & Camping Segovia, Corumbau s/n, T073-9986 2305, www.corumbaunet.com.br. There are only 5 small, fan-cooled and barely furnished chalets in this little family-run guesthouse close to the beach. They include breakfast and there are plots for camping out back.

Caravelas p79

$$ Marina Porto Abrolhos, R da Baleia, 5 km outside of town, T073-3674 1060, www.marinaportoabrolhos.com.br. One of the most comfortable hotels in the region, with a range of individual and family suites housed in faux-Polynesian chalets and gathered in a palm-tree garden around a large pool. Activities include trips to the Abrolhos.

$$ Pousada dos Navegantes, R das Palmeiras 45, Centre, T073-3297 1830, www.pousadanavegantes.com.br. Simple *pousada* with a pool near the beach organizing tours to the Abrolohos, dive excursions and dive certification. Friendly and helpful.

$$ Pousada Liberdade, Av Ministro Adalicio Nogueira 1551, Caravelas, T073-3297 2076, www.pousadaliberdade.com. br. Spacious but simple chalets in a large, lawned garden area next to a lake and just outside the town centre. Excursions organized to the Abrolhos Islands.

Restaurants

Arraial da Ajuda *p75, map p76*
Food in Arraial is pricey and restaurants tend to look better than the dishes they serve. There are numerous *barracas* selling simple seafood, juices and beer on Mucugê Beach, as well as the popular **Barraca de Pitinga** and **Barraca do Genésio** on Pitinga Beach.

$$$ Don Fabrizio, Estrada do Mucugê 402, T073-3575 1123. The best Italian in town, in an upmarket open air-restaurant with live music and reasonable wine.

$$$ Manguti, Estrada do Mucugê, T073-3575 2270, www.manguti.com.br. Reputedly the best in town, though the food looks like mutton dressed as lamb. Meat, pasta, fish served as comfort food alongside other Brazilian dishes. Very popular and informal.

$$$ Rosa dos Ventos, Alameda dos Flamboyants 24, T073-3575 1271. This romantic little spot decorated with arts and crafts by local artists cooks fresh food pulled from their own organic garden and the Atlantic. The menu is quite varied, with dishes like fish slow-roasted in banana leaf,

braised lamb and crawfish lobster (which should be ordered 24 hrs in advance).

$ Paulo Pescador, R São Bras 116, T073-3575 1242, www.paulopescador.com.br. One of the best options for lunch, with 6 different *pratos feitos* (set meals) to choose from and good fresh seafood. English spoken, good service. *Bobó de camarão* highly recommended. Very popular, there are often queues for tables.

Trancoso *p77*
Food in Trancoso is expensive. Those on a tight budget should shop at the supermarket between the main square and the new part of town. There are many fish restaurants in the *barracas* on the beach. Elba Ramalho, when in town, gigs at her restaurant, **Para Raio**.

$$$ Cacau, Quadrado 96, T073-3668 1296. The restaurant of choice for those who want to eat Bahian in Trancoso. The menu is strong on flavour and spices which includes starters like mini *acarajé* balls with *vatapá* or *caruru* and mains like *camarão nativo* (local prawns), served twitchingly fresh.

$$$ Capim Santo, R de Beco 55, Quadrado, T073-3668 4112, www.capimsanto.com.br. Paulistana ex-pat Sandra Marques' cooking is quintessentially Trancoso. Seafood dishes with a Bahian twist like prawn in manioc flour balls or tuna carpaccio are served under the stars by candlelight in a little tropical garden just off the Quadrado.

$$$ Maritaca, Quadrado, T073-3668 1258. A Marrakech theme may seem odd in hippy-chic Trancoso, but the sumptuous back deck at this new restaurant – with its open sky and beautiful drop-off view out to the sea – attracts a faithful cocktail crowd. The Italian food is adequate but lacks sparkle; slow service.

$$ Barraca Do Andrea, Coqueiros Beach. The most fashionable place to sip and sun. Run by a Sardinian who serves great Italian wood-fired pizza, super-fresh ceviche and a gamut of fruity caipirinhas and tropical juices.

$ Dona Maria, on a tiny little tile stall on the Quadrado in front of the Ainarí boutique. Before 0900. This joyful old lady and her grandson sell delicious home-baked bread, tiny prawn, chicken *empadas* (meat pies) and steaming hot treacle-sweet black coffee to fishermen (or visiting surfers) who rise with the sun.
$ Portinha, Quadrado. Good-value pay-by-weight options and a wealth of juices.

🎵 Bars and clubs

Arraial da Ajuda *p75, map p76*
Porto Seguro does not have much in the way of nightlife; most visitors stay in Arraial across the water. In Arraial, the *lambada* is danced at the **Jatobar** bar (in summer), by the church on the main square (opens 2300, *pensão* at the back is cheap, clean and friendly). **Limelight** has raves all year round. Many top Brazilian bands play at the beach clubs at **Praia do Parracho** in summer, entry is about US$20. Entry to other beach parties is about US$10.

🔵 What to do

Estação Veracel Veracruz *p75*
Ciro Albano, www.nebrazilbirding.com. The best birding guide for the northeast of Brazil offering tips to birding and wildlife sites, including Estação Veracruz, Canudos and the Chapada Diamantina.

Arraial da Ajuda *p75, map p76*
Portomondo, Ponta do Apaga Fogo 1, Marina Quinta do Porto Hotel, T073-3575 3686, www.portomondo.com. The best operator in southern Bahia with tours from around Trancoso, Caraíva and Corumbau to Monte Pascoal and Abrolhos. Excellent diving and ecotourism itineraries and car or helicopter transfers to hotels in Trancoso and further south.

Trancoso *p77*
Joáçio, T073-3668 1270, or ask at **Bouganvillea** restaurant on the main square. Good day trips to Espelho Beach, Caraíva and other beaches and forested areas in the area. Expect to pay US$10-15 per person depending on group size and distance.

Parque Nacional Marinho dos Abrolhos *p79*
See also Arriving in the Parque Nacional Marinho dos Abrolhos, page 80. All-inclusive trips from Porto Seguro can be arranged with **Portomondo** (see above). From Caravelas, book with **Abrolhos Turismo**, Praça Dr Emílio Imbassay 8, T073-3297 1149, www.abrolhosturismo.com. br or **Catamarã Veleiro Sanuk**, T073-3297 1344, www.catamarasanuk.cjb.net.

🔄 Transport

Porto Seguro *p72, map p72*
Air A taxi to the airport (T073-3288 1880) costs US$15. There are flights to **Belo Horizonte**, **Rio de Janeiro**, **Salvador**, **São Paulo** and **Ilhéus** in high season with GOL, www.voegol.com.br, Tam, www.tam.com. br, and Webjet, www.webjet.com.br.

Boat Boats cross the river to **Arraial da Ajuda** on the south bank, 5 mins, US$1 for foot passengers, US$5 for cars, every 15-30 mins day and night.

Bus During Brazilian holiday times, all transport should be booked well in advance. **Expresso Brasileiro** buses run from Praça dos Pataxós along the BR-367 stopping at the beaches north of town. Buses for Caraíva go via Eunápolis and Itabela (leaving Eunápolis at 1330, 2 hrs), or from Arraial D'Ajuda, via Trancoso daily at 0700 and 1600, extra bus at 1100 in high season (**Viação Águia Azul**, T073-3875 1170). To **Eunápolis**, 1 hr, US$5, very frequent. To **Curumuxatiba**, **Prado** and destinations further south, take a bus to Eunápolis, Texeira de Freitas or Itamaraju and an onward bus from there. To **Caraíva** buses leave at 0700, 1330 (high season) and 1500 (via Trancoso). To **Trancoso**, 2 daily buses, but easier to take the ferry to Arraial and catch one of the more frequent buses or *combis* from there. Other services via Eunápolis (those going north avoid Salvador) or **Itabuna** (5 hrs, US$25).

To **Rio de Janeiro**, daily, direct, 1745, US$80, *leito* US$70 (São Geraldo), 18 hrs (very cold a/c, take warm clothes); or take the 1800 to Ilhéus and change at Eunápolis. To **Belo Horizonte**, daily, direct, US$80 (São Geraldo). To **São Paulo**, direct, 1045, 25 hrs, not advisable, very slow; much better to go to Rio then take the Rio–São Paulo express. To **Salvador** (Águia Branca), daily, 12 hrs, US$80. To **Vitória**, daily, 11 hrs, US$60. To **Ilhéus**, daily 0730, 4½ hrs, US$45.

Car hire Several companies at the airport, including **Localiza**, T073-3288 1488 (and R Cova da Moça 620, T073-3288 1488), and **Nacional**, T073-3288 4291.

Cycle hire Oficina de Bicicleta, Av Getúlio Vargas e R São Pedro, US$15 for 24 hrs; also at Praça de Bandeira and at 2 de Julho 242.

Arraial da Ajuda *p75, map p76*
Ferry Take a bus or *combi* to Rio Buranhém, from where boats cross the river to **Porto Seguro**, on the north bank, 5 mins, US$1 for foot passengers, US$5 for cars, every 15-30 mins day and night.

Trancoso *p77*
Bus Buses run regularly on the newly paved road between Porto Seguro, Arraial d'Ajuda and Trancoso, at least every hour from Arraial in high season. To **Porto Seguro** US$4; to **Ajuda** US$2.40. Arriving from the south, change buses at Eunápolis from where the newly paved Linha Verde road runs to Trancoso. Buses for **Caraíva**

leave twice daily at 0800 and 1700, with an extra bus at 1200 in high season.

Caraíva *p78*
Access roads are poor and almost impossible after heavy rain. **Aguia Azul** buses run to **Porto Seguro** twice daily (3 times in high season), along a very poor dirt road involving a river crossing. If heading south, take a bus to **Itabela** or **Eunápolis** (0600, 3 hrs).

Parque Nacional de Monte Pascoal *p78*
To **Caraíva** there is a river crossing by boats which are always on hand. There is 1 bus a day Mon-Fri to **Itamaraju**, 16 km to the south.

Corumbau *p78*
Beach buggy taxis take you to the river crossing (US$40) to **Caraiva**, or it's about a 10-km walk. The punt ferry across the river costs around US$10. Buses run to **Itmaraju** and beyond to **Curumuxatiba**.

Caravelas *p79*
Air There are flights to **Belo Horizonte**, **São Paulo** and **Salvador**. Another option is to fly via **Porto Seguro**.

Bus Caravelas is well connected, with buses to **Texeira de Freitas** (4 a day), **Salvador**, **Nanuque**, **Itamaraju** and **Prado**.

Directory

Porto Seguro *p72, map p72*
Banks Agência do Descobrimento, Av Getúlio Vargas, also arranges flight tickets and house rental. Banco do Brasil, Av Beira Mar, 1000-1500, changes TCs and US$ cash, also Visa ATMs. Also at airport. Bradesco, Av Getulio Vargas, Visa ATMs. Deltur, in the new shopping centre, near Banco do Brasil. **Internet** Dotted throughout town. **Laundry** New Porto, Shopping Av, daily 0900-2230, priced per

item. **Post office** In the mini-shopping centre on the corner of R das Jandaias and Av dos Navegantes. **Telephone** Shopping Av, corner of Av dos Navegantes and Av Beira Mar, daily 0700-2300; also at Praça dos Pataxós, beside ferry terminal, daily 0700-2200, cheap rates after 2000.

Arraial da Ajuda *p75, map p76*
Banks There is a Banco do Brasil with a *câmbio* and ATM, and Bradesco and HSBC ATMs in the small shopping centre on Estrada do Mucugê. Several bars on Broadway change US$ cash, but rates are poor. **Internet** Dotted throughout

town. **Post office** Praça São Bras. **Telephone** Telemar on the main square, daily 0800-2200.

Trancoso *p77*
Banks Banco do Brasil ATM which only sometimes works with international Visa cards. Best to bring cash from Arraial. Most places accept TCs. **Internet** Several on the main square.

Caravelas *p79*
Banks The Banco do Brasil, Praça Dr Imbassahi, does not change money but has an ATM. There is also a Bradesco.

Linha Verde and the northern coast

Heading north from Salvador airport, the BA-099 coast road, or Estrada de Coco (Coconut Highway), passes many coconut plantations and 50 km of beautiful beaches. From south to north the best known are Ipitanga (famous for its reefs), Buraquinho, Jauá, Arembepe, Guarajuba, Itacimirim, Castelo Garcia D'Ávila (where there is a 16th-century fort) and Forte. North of the smart mini-resort town of Praia do Forte, the road is called the 'Linha Verde' (Green Line), which runs for 142 km to the Sergipe state border. The road is more scenic than the BR-101, especially near Conde. There are very few hotels or *pousadas* in the more remote villages. Among the most picturesque are Subaúma and Baixio; the latter, where the Rio Inhambupe meets the sea, is very beautiful. Buses serve most of these destinations.

Praia do Forte → *Phone code: 071.*
Some 80 km north of Salvador, is this pleasant mini-resort town much beloved of wealthy people from Salvador. Praia may no longer be a fishing village but it still feels low key. Aside from the town's main street, Alameda do Sol, most of the streets are sand. Much of the area around the town is protected, with turtle-nesting beaches, remnant coastal *restinga* forest, and a small area of marshland, which is home to a large number of birds, caymans and other animals. Birdwatching trips on the wetlands, which is home to many species of wading birds, spectacled caiman and capybara, are rewarding and can be organized through the town's large-scale 'eco' resort.

The **Projeto Tamar** ⓘ *Caixa Postal 2219, Rio Vermelho, Salvador, Bahia, T071-3876 1045, www.tamar.org.br*, is a national project that studies and preserves the sea turtles that lay their eggs in the area. Praia do Forte is the headquarters of the **National Turtle Preservation Programme** and is funded by the Worldwide Fund for Nature. There is a visitor centre at the project (US$1.50 for turtle sanctuary). The coast here is ideal for windsurfing and sailing, owing to constant fresh Atlantic breezes.

Praia do Forte takes its name from the castle built by a Portuguese settler, Garcia D'Avila, in 1556, to warn the city to the south of enemy invasion. He was given a huge area of land, from Praia do Forte to Maranhão, on which he made the first farm in Brazil. He brought the first herd of cattle to the country, cleared the virgin Atlantic forest and brought the first coconut and mango trees to Brazil.

Mangue Seco → *Phone code: 075.*

The last stop on the Linha Verde is Mangue Seco. The town was immortalized in Jorge Amado's book *Tieta*. A steep hill rises behind the village to white-sand dunes that offer superb views of the coast. The encroaching dunes have caused the mangrove to dry up.

The peninsula is connected to Pontal in the state of Sergipe by boat or canoe on the Rio Real (10-minute crossing). Buses run between Pontal and Estancia twice a day. The ferry across the river usually leaves before 1000 in the morning. A private launch will cost US$10, but it is usually possible to find someone to share the ride and cost.

Linha Verde and the northern coast listings

For hotel and restaurant price codes and other relevant information, see pages 8-11.

🛏 Where to stay

Praia do Forte *p89*

The town's main street had its name changed from Alameda do Sol to **Av ACM**. This street doesn't have numbers marked, so you just have to walk along to find your hotel. Prices rise steeply in the summer season. It may be difficult to find very cheap places to stay.

$$$$ Aloha Brasil Pousada, R da Aurora, T071-3676 0279, www.pousadaalohabrasil. com.br. Relaxing tropical garden and pool. Rooms are not big but are charming with king-sized beds and verandas.

$$$$ Porto Zarpa Hotel, R da Aurora, T071-3676 1414, www.portozarpa.com. br. Large 2-storey building surrounded by garden, close to the beach, cable TV, parking, pool, good for families.

$$$$ Praia do Forte Eco-Resort, Av do Farol, T071-3676 4000, www.praiadoforte ecoresort.com.br. A large-scale family resort set in tropical gardens on the beach and with programmes to visit the nearby protected areas. Beautiful pool.

$$$ Sobrado da Vila, Av ACM, T071-3676 1088, www.sobradodavila.com.br. The best in the village itself with a range of individually decorated rooms with balconies and a good-value restaurant, convenient for the town.

$$ Pousada João Sol, R da Corvina, T071-3676 1054, www.pousadajoaosol.com.br.

6 well-appointed and newly refurbished chalets. The owner speaks English, Spanish and German. Great breakfast.

$ Albergue da Juventude, Praia do Forte, R da Aurora 3, T071-3676 1094, www.albergue. com.br. Price per person. Smart youth hostel with decent shared rooms and rooms with en suites (**$$**), a large breakfast, fan, kitchen and shop, cheaper for HI members.

$ Pousada Tia Helena, just east of Praça dos Artistas, at Alameda das Estrelas, T071-3676 1198, T071-9901 2894 (mob), www. tiahelenapraiadoforte.com.br. Helena, the motherly proprietor, provides an enormous breakfast, simple rooms. Recently refurbished reductions for 3-day stays.

Mangue Seco *p23*

There are plenty of small cheap places along the seafront from the jetty, none with addresses or phone numbers (the village is tiny). There are simple restaurants around the main square next to the church. The beach has a handful of *barracas* serving cheap fish.

$$ Fantasias do Agreste, T075-3445 9011, www.pousadafantasiasdoagreste.com. Bright rooms with terraces overlooking a pool, decked out in tiled floors, whitewash and blocks of primary colour and furnished with wicker beds and light wood wardrobes.

$$ Village Mangue Seco, T075-3224 2965, www.villagemangueseco.com.br. Mock-adobe concrete chalets (some a/c, some fan-cooled), sitting around a pool in a large palm-shaded lawn dotted with tropical flowers.

🍴 Restaurants

Praia do Forte *p89*

\$\$ Bar Do Souza, Av do Sol, on the right as you enter the village. Best seafood in town, open daily, live music at weekends. Recommended.

\$\$ O Europeu, Av ACM, T071-3676 0232. Anglo-Brazilian owned, with the most adventurous menu in town with well-prepared homely dishes.

\$\$ Restaurante Casa da Nati, Av ACM, T071-3676 1239. Per kilo and Bahian food from a Praia do Forte local.

\$\$ Restaurante Point do Ivan, Av ACM, T071-9997 1711. Bahian food, good *moqueca*, *bobo de camarco* and cheap *prato feito*.

\$ Café Tango, Av ACM, T071-3676 1637. Pleasant open-air tea and coffee bar with great pastries and cakes.

🎯 What to do

Praia do Forte *p89*
Tour operators
Praia do Forte is ideal for windsurfing and sailing owing to constant fresh Atlantic breezes.
Odara Turismo, in the EcoResort Hotel, T071-3676 1080. Imaginative tours to surrounding areas and outlying villages and beaches using 4WD vehicles. They are very friendly and informative. Recommended. The owners, Norbert and Papy, speak English and German.

🚌 Transport

Praia do Forte *p89*
Bus It is easy to flag down buses from the crossroads on the main highway out of town. To get there take a *combi* (every 15 mins, US\$1) from town. Taxis are a rip-off. To **Salvador** buses run 5 times daily, 1 hr, US\$5 (**Santa Maria/Catuense**). To **Estancia** in Sergipe, 4-5 daily, US\$5.

Mangue Seco *p23*
Any Aracaju-bound bus will drop visitors at the town of **Estancia**, just across the border from Bahia in Sergipe state, from where there are 2 southbound buses a day to **Pontal** (a port comprising little more than a jetty, sitting opposite Mangue Seco) and more frequent Toyotas (leaving when full) from in front of the Estancia hospital. Infrequent slow boats cross the river from Pontal to Mangue Seco – usually 2-3 times daily. A private launch will cost US\$10-15, but there are invariably other people willing to share the boat and it is just a matter of waiting a while for them to turn up.

Chapada Diamantina and the sertão

The beautiful Chapada Diamantina National Park comprises a series of escarpments covered in Cerrado, *caatinga* and moist tropical forest, dripping with waterfalls and studded with caves. It is one of the highlights of inland Bahia. Although little of the forest is original, there is still plenty of wildlife including jaguar and maned wolf, and the area is good for birdwatching. Various trails cut through the park offering walks from a few hours to a few days, and many leave from the little colonial mining town of Lençóis, the ideal base for visiting the region.

The road from Salvador to Lençóis and the *chapada* passes through Feira de Santana, famous for its Micareta, an extremely popular out-of-season carnival. The harsh beauty of the *sertão* and its hospitable people are the reward for those wanting to get off the beaten track. The region has been scarred by droughts and a violent history of bandits, rebellions and religious leaders. Euclides da Cunha and Canudos are good places to start exploring this history. The Raso da Catarina, once a hiding place for Lampião, and the impressive Paulo Afonso waterfalls, can both be visited from the town of Paulo Afonso located on the banks of the São Francisco. This important river runs through the *sertão*, linking agricultural settlements such as Juazeiro, Ibotirama and Bom Jesus de Lapa and has its headwaters in northern Minas Gerais.

Lençóis and around → For listings, see pages 98-100. Phone code: 075. Population: 9000.

Lençóis is the best place from which to explore the *chapada*. It's a pretty little colonial village set on the banks of the fast-flowing Rio Lençóis, in the middle of the park. Many of the sights can be visited on foot from town. Lençóis was established as a mining town in 1844 and takes its name from the tents assembled by the prospectors who first arrived here (*lençóis* means 'white sheets' in Portuguese) set on the brown and green of the hillside. While there are still some *garimpeiros* (gold and diamond prospectors) left, tourism is now the main economic mainstay. Rather than precious metals, visitors are attracted by the cool climate, the relaxed atmosphere and the wonderful trekking in the Diamantina hills. The streets of Lençóis are lined with rustic houses, many of which are now *pousadas*, restaurants or shops selling quirky handicrafts and semi-precious stones.

Arriving in Lençóis The **airport** ① *20 km from town, Km 209, BR-242, T075-3625 8100,* has weekly Saturday flights to and from São Paulo via Salvador, with **TRIP** ① *www.voetrip. com.br.* There are direct buses from Salvador and other cities in Bahia via Feira de Santana. Buses from Recife and the northeast come via Seabra, west of Lençóis. There is a tourist office, **Sectur**, inside the market next to the river.

Lençóis

Where to stay 🛏
Camping &
  Pousada Lumiar 1
Canto das Aguas 2
Casa de Geleia 3
Casa de Hélia 4
Estalagem de Alcino 5
Lençóis 6
Pousada dos Duendes 7
Pousada Vila Serrano 8
Pousada Violeiro 9

Restaurants 🍴
Artistas de Massa 1
Cozinha Aberta 2
Gaya 3
Neco's 4

Bars & clubs 🍸
Fazedinha e Tal 5

Excursions from Lençóis

On walking trips from Lençóis it is possible to visit the *serrano* (in the hills above town), which has wonderful natural pools in the river bed that give a great spring-water massage when you sit under them; or the **Salão de Areia**, where the coloured sands for the bottle paintings come from. **Ribeirão do Meio** is a 45-minute walk from town; here locals slide down a long natural water chute into a big pool (it is best to watch someone else first and take something to slide in). Also near Lençóis are two very pretty waterfalls: the **Cachoeira da Primavera**; and the **Cachoeira Sossego**, a picture-postcard cascade plunging into a deep blue pool.

Other towns in the chapada

There is simple accommodation and a handful of tour operators in **Palmeiras**, some 55 km west of Lençóis. The town makes a far quieter alternative base for exploring the *chapada*. *Combis* run sporadically between Palmeiras and Lençóis. **Mucugê** town in the far south, 134 km from Lençóis is sleepier still, and has a fascinating whitewash cemetery filled with elaborate mausoleums and set against the dark granite of the hillside. There are bus connections with Lençóis and Feira de Santana. The adjacent **Parque Municipal de Mucugê** was set up to protect the *sempre viva* or *chuveirinho* plant – a beautiful globe of white flowers whose popularity with flower arrangers in Brazil almost led to their extinction in the late 20th century. **Igatu** has a population of approximately 350 people, some of them live in the largely abandoned stone houses built into or around Cyclopean boulders that dot the landscape. Wandering around the village and the ruins is a haunting experience. There are two *pousadas* in the village.

Parque Nacional da Chapada Diamantina → *For listings, see pages 98-100.*

The Chapada Diamantina National Park was founded in 1985 and comprises 1500 sq km of escarpment broken by extensive tracts of *caatinga* scrub forest, Cerrado, patches of moist Atlantic coast forest and pântano (wetlands with permanent plant growth). The diverse ecosystems have an associated diversity of flora and fauna. There is very little primary forest left, but the area is nonetheless home to rare large mammals such as maned wolf, jaguar and ocelot and birds endemic to all of the ecosystems. Spectaculars include the king vulture, crowned eagle, red-legged seriema and blue-winged macaw. There are birding guides available in Lençóis (see page 99).

Arriving in the Parque Nacional da Chapada Diamantina

The **park headquarters** ① *R Barão do Rio Branco 25, Palmeiras, T075-3332 2420*, is 50 km from Lençóis. However, Lençóis is a much more practical source of information and the numerous agencies make it easy to find out what's what. See also www.infochapada.com.

Roy Funch, an American who used to manage the park and who now offers guided walks (see page 99), has written an excellent book on the *chapada*: *A Visitor's Guide to the Chapada Diamantina Mountains* (Collection Apoio 45), in English and Portuguese. The book includes history and geology of the region, an itinerary of all the principal sights, with instructions on how to reach them and a thorough, though not comprehensive, checklist of birds and mammals. It is widely available in Lençóis.

Background

The *chapada* forms part of the Brazilian shield, one of the oldest geological formations on earth, dating from the when the world was only one land mass. It extends north into the Serra da Capivara and Jalapão, and south into the Serra do Espinhaço and Serra da Canastra in Minas and the mountains of Mato Grosso and northern Bolivia.

Cave paintings and petroglyphs suggest that people have been living in and around the *chapada* for millennia. However, there were no permanent settlers in the hills in recorded history until the arrival of Portuguese prospectors in the 1700s, who discovered gold and diamonds in the extreme south of the *chapada* near Livramento de Nossa Senhora and in the north near Jacobina. The Portuguese kept the findings secret for fear of driving down world gem prices, and ceding the *chapada* to other European powers, notably the Dutch and Spanish, who were invading and occupying Brazilian territory repeatedly during this period.

Chapada Diamantina

The *chapada* didn't open up fully to mining until 1844, when Mucugê, Rio de Contas and subsequently Lençóis were founded and settled by miners from neighbouring Minas Gerais and western Bahia, followed by Portuguese noblemen from the Bahian coast. The latter evolved into *coroneis*: robber barons who set-up ruthless local fiefdoms run by gun-toting *jangada* henchmen. The most famous was Horácio de Mattos, a prototype for many modern-day rural Brazilian politicians. De Mattos sucked all the money out of the *chapada* with his personal campaigns. He carried out famous vendettas against two other *coroneis*, Manuel Fabrício de Oliveira and Militão Rodrigues Coelho, to establish patriarchal dominance, overthrew the state government, routed the federal army and chased the infamous communist Prestes column all the way across Brazil and into Bolivia. He was arrested in Salvador in 1930 and assassinated in mysterious circumstances the following year.

Visiting the park

The *chapada* is cut by dirt roads, trails and rivers, which lead to waterfalls, viewpoints on table-top mountains, caves and natural swimming holes. There are many different hikes, and many of the routes have been used for centuries by the local farmers and miners, but finding your own way is difficult and it is best to visit on a guided trip.

There are more than 24 tour operators in Lençóis and organizing a trip to even the most distant sights is straightforward. Most tours tend to be car-based and rather sedentary as these are more profitable. But there are plenty of great hikes and sights around Lençóis, so consider all the options before signing up. Brazilian tourists are often more interested in chatting loudly among themselves than in hearing the quiet music of nature, so it can be difficult to see wildlife. ►► *See What to do, page 99.*

The most impressive sights in the *chapada* are included in the standard packages; most have an entrance fee. Trips include the extensive **Gruta da Lapa Doce** (US$5) and **Pratinha caves** (US$5); the latter are cut through by glassy blue water. The table-top mountains at the **Morro de Pai Inácio**, US$2, 30 km from Lençóis, offer the best view of the *chapada*, especially at sunset. The 384-m-high **Cachoeira da Fumaça** (Smoke or Glass Waterfall) is the second highest in Brazil and lies deeper within the park 2½ hours' hike from the village of **Capão**. The view is astonishing; the updraft of the air currents often makes the water flow back up creating the 'smoke' effect. The **Rio Marimbus** flows through and area of semi-swamp reminiscent of the Pantanal and is very rich in birdlife; whilst the **Rio Mucugezinho** plunges over the blood-red **Cachoeira do Diabo** in an extensive area of Cerrado just below the craggy **Roncador** ('snorer') waterfall.

Hiking in the chapada

It is essential to use a guide for treks as it is easy to get lost. Trail-walking in the park can involve clambering over rocks and stepping stones so bring strong shoes. A reasonable level of physical fitness is advisable. There are a lot of mosquitos in campsites so carry repellent. For overnight trips it is highly advisable to bring a fleece and sleeping bag as nights in the 'winter' months can be cold. Sometimes, guides can arrange these. A tent is useful but optional; although many camps are beside reasonably hospitable caves. Torches (flashlights) and a water bottle are essentials.

The **Morro do Pai Inacio to Capão** trail is a 25-km day hike that leads from the summit of the Pai Inácio escarpment around other table-top mountains, passing through Cerrado, *caatinga* and arable areas to the Capão Valley. Another day hike is from **Lençóis to Capão**, along a series of rivers (great for swimming) and around the base of the mountains, with a car ride back at the end of the walk.

The **Cachoeira da Fumaça** trail leaves direct from Lençóis and takes two to three days to reach the base of the falls, from where there is a steep hike to the top. If you only have one day, it's possible to drive the 70 km to the **Vale do Capão** and hike the steep 6-km trail to the top of the falls. Both trails are very popular in high season.

A trail runs from **Igatu to Andaraí**, leaving from the central square of the former town past the cemetery and following the Xique-Xique River. The walk takes four hours and offers wonderful views of the mountain landscape. There are plenty of river bank stops for a cooling swim. There are longer treks too.

The **Vale do Paty** hike is a four- to six-day walk running through the heart of the *serra* along a valley surrounded by imposing *meseta* table-top mountains. There are many good stopping places with viewpoints, caves, swimming holes and waterfalls. The route usually departs from Capão in the north or from the village of Guiné just west of Andaraí town.

For a full cross-section of the park, hike the 112-km **Travessia Diamantina**, which runs from the Vale do Capão in the north across the park via the Vale do Paty, to the Cachoeira do Buracão in the far south. Accommodation is in tents and rustic *pousadas* and there are side trips to the Cachoeira da Fumaça (near Capão), Igatu, Poço Encatado, and the Marimbus Pantanal area and Roncador falls. Establish which sights you want to visit before setting off.

The sertão → *For listings, see pages 98-100.*

Most of Bahia is arid: a rock and scrub semi-desert covered in leafless *caatinga* forest, cut by the blue vein of the majestic Rio São Francisco and dotted with little settlements where local people scratch a meagre living from the sun-baked earth. This is the *sertão* – a backland that has produced some of Brazil's most enduring mythical figures. **Antônio Conselheiro**, a purple-robed desert prophet whose rag-tag band of marauders and bandits converted to Christianity in the late 19th-century and built Canudos, crushed two armies and almost broke the Brazilian state. **Lampião** – the *sertão's* brutal Robin Hood – pillaged the rich *coroneis*, distributed wealth and brutal justice to the desert villages in the early 20th century and died in a gun battle in a town famous for its troubadours and poets. Their legacy, the iron hand of *coroneis* who impose rough justice to this day and countless forgotten, timeless festivals and rites still characterize the dust and dirt towns of this vast interior. Tourists are seldom seen and are always a curiosity.

Euclides da Cunha and Monte Santo → *Phone code: 075.*
North of Feira da Santana, at Km 225 on the BR-116 road to Fortaleza, **Euclides da Cunha**, is a good base for exploring the Canudos area with a couple of standard hotels. The *rodoviária* is on the BR-116, T075-3271 1365.

About 38 km west is the famous hill shrine of **Monte Santo** in the *sertão*, reached by 3.5 km of steps cut into the rocks of the **Serra do Picaraça**. It's a 45-minute walk each way, so set off early. This is the scene of pilgrimages and great religious devotion during **Holy Week**. The shrine was built by an Italian who had a vision of the cross on the mountain in 1765. One block north of the bottom of the stairs is the **Museu do Sertão**, with pictures from the 1897 Canudos rebellion.

Canudos → *Phone code: 075.*
Canudos itself is 100 km away. Religious rebels, led by Antônio Conselheiro, defeated three expeditions sent against them in 1897 before being overwhelmed. The Rio Vaza Barris, which runs through Canudos, has been dammed, and the town has been moved to **Nova Canudos** by the dam. Part of the old town is still located 10 km west in the **Parque Estadual de Canudos**, created in 1997.

The 1500-ha **Estação Biológica de Canudos** lies a few kilometres from the state park. It was founded in 1989 by the **Fundação Biodiversitas** (www.biodiversitas.org.br) to protect the only remaining nesting sites of the critically endangered giant blue Lear's macaw. Fewer than 100 birds nest here, on a large sun-baked clay cliff within the reserve. The park and reserve can only be visited with a hire car, or by taxi from Canudos town. The Estação Biológica de Canudos can also be visited on a birding tour with guides such as **Ciro Albano** (see page 100). There are direct buses to Canudos from Salvador. For tourist information see www.canudosnet.com.br.

For hotel and restaurant price codes and other relevant information, see pages 8-11.

🛏 Where to stay

Lençóis *p93, map p93*

$$$$ Canto das Águas, Av Senhor dos Passos, T075-3334 1154, www.lencois. com.br. Medium-sized riverside hotel with modest a/c or fan-cooled rooms, a pool and efficient service. The best rooms are in the new wing; others can be musty.

$$$ Hotel de Lençóis, R Altinha Alves 747, T075-3334 1102, www.hoteldelencois. com. br. Plain, dark wood and white- tiled rooms with terracotta roofs set in a handsome colonial house in a grassy garden on the edge of the park. Good breakfast, pool and a restaurant.

$$$ Pousada Vila Serrano, R Alto do Bonfim 8, T075-3334 1486, www. vilaserrano.com.br. Warm and welcoming mock-colonial *pousada* overlooking a patio and little garden 5 mins from town. Excellent service, breakfast, trips organized. Very friendly and knowledgeable.

$$ Estalagem de Alcino, R Gen Viveiros de Morais 139, T075-3334 1171, www. alcino estalagem.com. An enchanting and beautifully restored period house with a range of rooms furnished with 19th-century antiques.

$ Casa da Geleia, R Gen Viveiros 187, T075-3334 1151. A handful of smart chalets set in a huge garden at the entrance to the town. English spoken, good breakfast, including sumptuous jams and honeys made or collected by the owner. Zé Carlos is a keen birdwatcher and an authority on the region.

$ Casa de Hélia, R da Muritiba, T075-3334 1143, www.casadehelia.com.br. Attractive and welcoming little guesthouse. English spoken. Good facilities, legendary breakfast.

$ HI Lençóis, R Boa Vista 121, T075-3334 1497, www.hostelchapada.com.br. A large, friendly and well-run hostel with an adventure sports agency in one of the town's grand old colonial houses. The building has been completely restored and has singles, en suite doubles and single-sex 4- to 6-bed dorms; shared kitchen and a large, airy garden with hammocks and littered with outdoor chairs.

$ Pousada dos Duendes, R do Pires, T075-3334 1229, www.pousadadosduendes. com. Run by English Olivia Taylor and often crowded with backpackers. Rooms are basic with shared showers, modest breakfast and dinner (with veggie options). Their tour agency, **H2O Expeditions**, arranges tours and treks from 1 to 11 days. Check with other agencies in town before committing.

$ Pousada Violeiro, R Prof Assis 70, T075-3334 1259, www.pousadavioleiro.com. br. Very simple rooms with room for up to 4 just behind the bus stop near the river. Quiet and conservative.

Camping

Camping and Pousada Lumiar, near the Rosário church in the town centre, T075-3334 1241. A large grassy area for pitching tents and a series of very simple rooms and bungalows. Popular restaurant. Friendly.

Euclides da Cunha and Monte Santo
p97

$$ Do Conselheiro, Av Mcal Juarez Tavora 187, Euclides, T075-3275 1814. Standard town hotel with breakfast in the price.

$$ Grapiuna, Praça Monsenhor Berenguer 401, Euclides, T075-3275 1157. Basic rooms with a/c and cheaper options without bath. Recommended.

Canudos *p97*

$ Brasil, Nova Canudos. Very simple rooms with en suites and fans. Cheaper without breakfast.

🍴 Restaurants

Lençóis *p93, map p93*
\$\$\$ Cozinha Aberta, Rui Barbosa 42, just east of the main *praça*, T075-3334 1309, www.cozinhaaberta.com.br. The best in town with organic and slow food from Paulistana chef Deborah Doitschinoff.
\$\$ Artistas da Massa, R Miguel Calmon. Italian dishes, mainly pasta and pizza.
\$\$ Neco's, Praça Maestro Clarindo Pachêco 15, T075-3334 1179. Set meal of local dishes of the kind once eaten by the *garimpeiro* miners, such as saffron-stewed mutton accompanied by prickly pear cactus, crisp, tart *batata da terra* and fried green banana.
\$ Gaya, Praça Horácio Matos s/n, T075-3334 1167. Organic and wholefood with large salads generous juices and sandwiches. The owners organize trips into the *chapada*.

🍸 Bars and clubs

Lençóis *p93, map p93*
Clube Sete, R das Pedras. Little dance club open Fri and Sat nights.
Doce Barbaros, R das Pedras, 21. Lively little bar almost any night of the week.
Fazendinha e Tal, R das Pedras 125. Very popular bar with rustic *garimpeiro* decoration serving hundreds of different *cachacas*.

🛍 Shopping

Lençóis *p93, map p93*
There is a little market in the main square selling arts and crafts.
Instrumentos, R das Pedras 78, T075-3334 1334. Unusual faux-Brazilian and African musical instruments by quirky ex-pat Argentinian Jorge Fernando.
Zambumbeira, R das Pedras at Tamandare, T075-3334 1207. Beautiful ceramics by reknowned artisans like Zé Caboclo, jewellery, walking sticks and arty bric-a-brac.

🎯 What to do

Lençóis *p93, map p93*
Guides offer their services at most *pousadas* (about US\$20-30 per trip); most of them are very young. The following are recommended:
Chapada Adventure, Av 7 de Setembro 7, T075-3334 2037, www.chapadaadventure.com.br. A small operator offering good-value car-based tours and light hiking throughout the *chapada*.
Edmilson (known as Mil), R Domingos B Souza 70, T075-3334 1319. Knowledgeable and reliable guide who knows the region extremely well.
For a da Trilha, R das Pedras 202, www.foradatrilha.com.br. Longer hikes and light adventures, from canyoning to rapelling.
Gaya, Praça Horácio Matos s/n (see Restaurants), T075-3334 1167, T075-9992 2820 (mob), rafa.gaya@yahoo.com.br. Rafa organizes budget backpacker trips in and around the *chapada* in an old Toyota Bandeirante. Tours cost around US\$200 for 300-km round trips for up to 10 people, and include unusual locations such as the Cachoeira do Mosquito. Book ahead if possible.
Luiz Krug, contact via Vila Serrano, T075-3334 1102. An independent, English-speaking guide specializing in geology and caving.
Roy Funch, T075-3334 1305, www.fcd.org.br. The ex-director of the Chapada Diamantina National Park is an excellent guide and has written a visitors' guide to the park in English. It is recommended as the best for information on history, geography and trails of the *chapada*. Highly recommended. He can also be booked through www.elabrasil.com.
Trajano, contact via **Vila Serrano** or **Casa da Hélia**, T075-3334 1143. Speaks English and Hebrew and is a good-humoured guide for treks to the bottom of the Cachoeira da Fumaça.

Venturas e Aventuras, Praça Horácio
de Matos 20, T075-3334 1304. Excellent
trekking expeditions, up to 6 days.
Zé Carlos, T075-3334 1151, contact
through **Casa da Geleia** or **Vila Serrano**.
The best guide for birdwatching.

Canudos *p97*
Alternative therapies
The *chapada* is a centre for alternative
treatments. All the practitioners listed come
highly recommended.
Anita Marti, T075-9989 8328. Healing and
therapeutic massage and treatments.
Dieter Herzberg, T075-9984 2720,
dieterherzberg@yahoo.com.br. All manner
of therapeutic and healing massage.
Jaques Gagnon, T075-3334 1281, www.
janeladaalma.com. Neuro-structural
therapy and healing massage.

Birdwatching
Ciro Albano, www.nebrazilbirding.com.
The best birding guide for the northeast of
Brazil offering tips to birding and wildlife
sites, including Estação Veracruz, Canudos
and the Chapada Diamantina.

⊖ Transport

Lençóis *p93, map p93*
Air Airport, Km 209, BR-242, 20 km
from town T075-3625 8100. Weekly
flights from **São Paulo** and **Salvador**
with **TRIP** (www.voetrip.com.br).

Bus Real Expresso to **Salvador** 3 a day,
US$24, *comercial* via Feira de Santana.
Book in advance, especially at weekends
and holidays. For the rest of Bahia state
change at Feira de Santana; it is not
necessary to go via Salvador. Buses also to
Recife, Ibotirama, Barreiras or **Palmas**
(for Jalapão), **Chapada dos Veadeiros** and
Brasília, 16 hrs, US$60 (all with transfer in
Seabra, several buses daily).

Canudos *p97*
At least 4 buses daily leave Salvador's
rodoviária for the city of **Euclides da
Cunha**. From here there are regular
connections to Canudos. Taxis in Canudos
town can be hired for a full day for around
US$40.

❶ Directory

Lençóis *p93, map p93*
Banks and post office There is a
Bradesco with an ATM, and a post office
(Mon-Fri 0900-1700) on the main square.

Contents

Footnotes

Basic Portuguese for travellers

Learning Portuguese is a useful part of the preparation for a trip to Brazil and no volume of dictionaries, phrase books or word lists will provide the same enjoyment as being able to communicate directly with the people of the country you are visiting. It is a good idea to make an effort to grasp the basics before you go. As you travel you will pick up more of the language and the more you know, the more you will benefit from your stay.

General pronunciation

Within Brazil itself, there are variations in pronunciation, intonation, phraseology and slang. This makes for great richness and for the possibility of great enjoyment in the language. A couple of points which the newcomer to the language will spot immediately are the use of the tilde (~) over 'a' and 'o'. This makes the vowel nasal, as does a word ending in 'm' or 'ns', or a vowel followed by 'm' + consonant, or by 'n' + consonant. Another important point of spelling is that for words ending in 'i' and 'u' the emphasis is on the last syllable, though (unlike Spanish) no accent is used. This is especially relevant in place names like Buriti, Guarapari, Caxambu, Iguaçu. Note also the use of 'ç', which changes the pronunciation of c from hard [k] to soft [s].

Personal pronouns

In conversation, most people refer to 'you' as *você*, although in the south and in Pará *tu* is more common. To be more polite, use *O Senhor/A Senhora*. For 'us', *gente* (people, folks) is very common when it includes you too.

Portuguese words and phrases

Greetings and courtesies

hello	*oi*	how are you?	*como vai você tudo bem?/tudo bom?*
good morning	*bom dia*		
good afternoon	*boa tarde*	I am fine	*vou bem/tudo bem*
good evening/night	*boa noite*	pleased to meet you	*um prazer*
goodbye	*adeus/tchau*	no	*não*
see you later	*até logo*	yes	*sim*
please	*por favor/faz favor*	excuse me	*com licença*
thank you	*obrigado* (if a man is speaking)/ *obrigada* (if a woman is speaking)	I don't understand	*não entendo*
		please speak slowly	*fale devagar por favor*
		what is your name?	*qual é seu nome?*
		my name is …	*o meu nome é …*
thank you very much	*muito obrigado/ muito obrigada*	go away!	*vai embora!*

Basic questions

where is?	*onde está/* *onde fica?*	when?	*quando?*
		I want to go to …	*quero ir para …*
why?	*por que?*	when does the bus	*a que hor sai/*
how much does it cost?	*quanto custa?*	leave?/arrive?	*chega o ônibus?*
what for?	*para que?*	is this the way to	*aquí é o caminho*
how much is it?	*quanto é?*	the church?	*para a igreja?*
how do I get to … ?	*para chegar a … ?*		

Basics

bathroom/toilet	*banheiro*	notes/coins	*notas/moedas*
police (policeman)	*a polícia (o polícia)*	cash	*dinheiro*
hotel	*o (a pensão,*	breakfast	*o caféde manh*
	a hospedaria)	lunch	*o almoço*
restaurant	*o restaurante*	dinner/supper	*o jantar*
	(o lanchonete)	meal	*a refeição*
post office	*o correio*	drink	*a bebida*
telephone office	*(central) telefônica*	mineral water	*a água mineral*
supermarket	*o supermercado*	soft fizzy drink	*o refrigerante*
market	*o mercado*	beer	*a cerveja*
bank	*o banco*	without sugar	*sem açúcar*
bureau de change	*a casa de câmbio*	without meat	*sem carne*
exchange rate	*a taxa de câmbio*		

Getting around

on the left/right	*à esquerda/*	flight	*o vôa*
	à direita	first/second class	*primeira/*
straight on	*direto*		*segunda clase*
to walk	*caminhar*	train station	*a ferroviária*
bus station	*a rodoviária*	combined bus and	*a rodoferroviária*
bus	*o ônibus*	train station	
bus stop	*a parada*	ticket	*o passagem/*
train	*a trem*		*o bilhete*
airport	*o aeroport*	ticket office	*a bilheteria*
aeroplane/airplane	*o avião*		

Accommodation

room	*quarto*	hot/cold water	*água quente/fria*
noisy	*barulhento*	to make up/clean	*limpar*
single/double room	*(quarto de) solteiro/*	sheet(s)	*o lençol (os lençóis)*
	(quarto para) casal	blankets	*as mantas*
room with two beds	*quarto com*	pillow	*o travesseiro*
	duas camas	clean/dirty towels	*as toalhas limpas/*
with private bathroom	*quarto com*		*sujas*
	banheiro	toilet paper	*o papel higiêico*

Health

chemist	*a farmacia*	condoms	*as camisinhas/*
doctor	*o coutor/a doutora*		*os preservativos*
(for) pain	*(para) dor*	contraceptive (pill)	*anticoncepional*
stomach	*o esômago (a barriga)*		*(a pílula)*
head	*a cabeça*	period	*a menstruação/*
fever/sweat	*a febre/o suor*		*a regra*
	higiênicas	sanitary towels/	*toalhas absorventes/*
diarrhoea	*a diarréia*	tampons	*absorventes internos*
blood	*o sangue*	contact lenses	*lentes de contacto*

Time

at one o'clock	*a uma hota*	it's twenty past six/	*são seis e vinte*
(am/pm)	*(da manhã/da tarde)*	six twenty	
at half past two/	*as dois e meia*	it's five to nine	*são cinco para as nove*
two thirty		in ten minutes	*em dez minutos*
at a quarter to three	*quinze para as três*	five hours	*cinco horas*
it's one o'clock	*é uma*	does it take long?	*sura muito?*
it's seven o'clock	*são sete horas*		

Days

Monday	*segunda feiro*	Friday	*sexta feira*
Tuesday	*terça feira*	Saturday	*sábado*
Wednesday	*quarta feira*	Sunday	*domingo*
Thursday	*quinta feira*		

Months

January	*janeiro*	July	*julho*
February	*fevereiro*	August	*agosto*
March	*março*	September	*setembro*
April	*abril*	October	*outubro*
May	*maio*	November	*novembro*
June	*junho*	December	*dezembro*

Numbers

one	*um/uma*	twelve	*doze*
two	*dois/duas*	thirteen	*treze*
three	*três*	fourteen	*catorze*
four	*quatro*	fifteen	*quinze*
five	*cinco*	sixteen	*dezesseis*
six	*seis* ('*meia*' half, is	seventeen	*dezessete*
	frequently used for	eighteen	*dezoito*
	number 6 ie half-dozen)	nineteen	*dezenove*
seven	*sete*	twenty	*vinte*
eight	*oito*	twenty-one	*vente e um*
nine	*nove*	thirty	*trinta*
ten	*dez*	forty	*cuarenta*
eleven	*onze*	fifty	*cinqüe*

sixty	*sessenta*	ninety	*noventa*
seventy	*setenta*	hundred	*cem, cento*
eighty	*oitenta*	thousand	*mil*

Useful slang

that's great/cool	*que legal*	cheesy/tacky	*brega*
bloke/guy/geezer	*cara* (literally 'face')	posh, spoilt girl/boy	*patricinha/mauricinho*
biker slang for	*mano*	with rich parents	
bloke/guy		in fashion/cool	*descolado*

Glossary

azulejo	tile
baía	bay
bairro	area or suburb
bandas	marching bands that compete during Carnaval
bandeirantes	early Brazilian conquistadors who went on missions to open up the interior
barraca	beach hut or stall
berimbau	stringed instrument that accompanies capoeira
biblioteca	library
bilhete	ticket
botequim	small bar, open-air
caboclo	rural workers of mixed descent
cachaça	cane liquor
cachoeira	waterfall
caipirinha	Brazilian cocktail, made from *cachaça*, lime, sugar and ice
câmbio	bureau de change
candomblé	African-Brazilian religion
capela	chapel
capoeira	African-Brazilian martial art
Carioca	person from Rio de Janeiro
carnaval	carnival
cerrado	scubland
cerveja	beer
churrascaria	barbecue restaurant, often all-you-can-eat
empadas	mini pasties
estrada	road
favela	slum/shanty town
fazenda	country estate or ranch
feijoada	black-bean stew
ferroviária	train station
forró	music and dance style from northeast Brazil
frevo	frenetic musical style from Recife
gaúcho	cowboy, especially from Rio Grande do Sul
garimpeiro	miner or prospector
igreja	church
ilha	island
jangada	small fishing boats, peculiar to the northeast
jardim	garden
lanchonete	café/deli
largo	small square
leito	executive bus
litoral	*coast/coastal area*
mata	jungle
mercado	market
Mineiro	person from Minas Gerais
mirante	viewpoint
mosteiro	monastery
Paulista	person from São Paulo
ponte	bridge
praça	square/plaza
praia	beach
prancha	surfboard
prefeitura	town hall
rio	river
rodoviária	bus station
rua	street
sambaquis	archaeological shell mounds
sertão	arid interior of the northeast
Sertanejo	person who lives in the *sertão*
vaqueiro	cowboy in the north

Acronyms and official names

FUNAI	Fundacao Nacional do Indio (National Foundation for Indigenous People)
IBAMA	Instituto Brasileiro do Meio Ambiente E Dos Recursos Naturais Renováveis (Brazilian Institute of Environment and Renewable Natural Resources)
MPB	Música Popular Brasileira
RAMSAR	Wetlands Convention

Notes

Notes

Notes

Index

Titles available in the Footprint *Focus* range

Latin America	UK RRP	US RRP
Bahia & Salvador	£7.99	$11.95
Brazilian Amazon	£7.99	$11.95
Brazilian Pantanal	£6.99	$9.95
Buenos Aires & Pampas	£7.99	$11.95
Cartagena & Caribbean Coast	£7.99	$11.95
Costa Rica	£8.99	$12.95
Cuzco, La Paz & Lake Titicaca	£8.99	$12.95
El Salvador	£5.99	$8.95
Guadalajara & Pacific Coast	£6.99	$9.95
Guatemala	£8.99	$12.95
Guyana, Guyane & Suriname	£5.99	$8.95
Havana	£6.99	$9.95
Honduras	£7.99	$11.95
Nicaragua	£7.99	$11.95
Northeast Argentina & Uruguay	£8.99	$12.95
Paraguay	£5.99	$8.95
Quito & Galápagos Islands	£7.99	$11.95
Recife & Northeast Brazil	£7.99	$11.95
Rio de Janeiro	£8.99	$12.95
São Paulo	£5.99	$8.95
Uruguay	£6.99	$9.95
Venezuela	£8.99	$12.95
Yucatán Peninsula	£6.99	$9.95

Asia	UK RRP	US RRP
Angkor Wat	£5.99	$8.95
Bali & Lombok	£8.99	$12.95
Chennai & Tamil Nadu	£8.99	$12.95
Chiang Mai & Northern Thailand	£7.99	$11.95
Goa	£6.99	$9.95
Gulf of Thailand	£8.99	$12.95
Hanoi & Northern Vietnam	£8.99	$12.95
Ho Chi Minh City & Mekong Delta	£7.99	$11.95
Java	£7.99	$11.95
Kerala	£7.99	$11.95
Kolkata & West Bengal	£5.99	$8.95
Mumbai & Gujarat	£8.99	$12.95

Africa & Middle East	UK RRP	US RRP
Beirut	£6.99	$9.95
Cairo & Nile Delta	£8.99	$12.95
Damascus	£5.99	$8.95
Durban & KwaZulu Natal	£8.99	$12.95
Fès & Northern Morocco	£8.99	$12.95
Jerusalem	£8.99	$12.95
Johannesburg & Kruger National Park	£7.99	$11.95
Kenya's Beaches	£8.99	$12.95
Kilimanjaro & Northern Tanzania	£8.99	$12.95
Luxor to Aswan	£8.99	$12.95
Nairobi & Rift Valley	£7.99	$11.95
Red Sea & Sinai	£7.99	$11.95
Zanzibar & Pemba	£7.99	$11.95

Europe	UK RRP	US RRP
Bilbao & Basque Region	£6.99	$9.95
Brittany West Coast	£7.99	$11.95
Cádiz & Costa de la Luz	£6.99	$9.95
Granada & Sierra Nevada	£6.99	$9.95
Languedoc: Carcassonne to Montpellier	£7.99	$11.95
Málaga	£5.99	$8.95
Marseille & Western Provence	£7.99	$11.95
Orkney & Shetland Islands	£5.99	$8.95
Santander & Picos de Europa	£7.99	$11.95
Sardinia: Alghero & the North	£7.99	$11.95
Sardinia: Cagliari & the South	£7.99	$11.95
Seville	£5.99	$8.95
Sicily: Palermo & the Northwest	£7.99	$11.95
Sicily: Catania & the Southeast	£7.99	$11.95
Siena & Southern Tuscany	£7.99	$11.95
Sorrento, Capri & Amalfi Coast	£6.99	$9.95
Skye & Outer Hebrides	£6.99	$9.95
Verona & Lake Garda	£7.99	$11.95

North America	UK RRP	US RRP
Vancouver & Rockies	£8.99	$12.95

Australasia	UK RRP	US RRP
Brisbane & Queensland	£8.99	$12.95
Perth	£7.99	$11.95

For the latest books, e-books and a wealth of travel information, visit us at: www.footprinttravelguides.com.

 footprinttravelguides.com

 Join us on facebook for the latest travel news, product releases, offers and amazing competitions: www.facebook.com/footprintbooks.